Pedagogy of the Depressed

T0316283

Also by the Author

The Textual Life of Airports: Reading the Culture of Flight (2011)
Deconstructing Brad Pitt (2014), co-edited with Robert Bennett
The End of Airports (2015)
Airportness: The Nature of Flight (2017)
The Work of Literature in an Age of Post-Truth (2018)
*Searching for the Anthropocene: A Journey into the Environmental
Humanities* (2019)

Pedagogy of the Depressed

Christopher Schaberg

BLOOMSBURY ACADEMIC
NEW YORK · LONDON · OXFORD · NEW DELHI · SYDNEY

BLOOMSBURY ACADEMIC
Bloomsbury Publishing Inc
1385 Broadway, New York, NY 10018, USA
50 Bedford Square, London, WC1B 3DP, UK
29 Earlsfort Terrace, Dublin 2, Ireland

BLOOMSBURY, BLOOMSBURY ACADEMIC and the Diana logo are trademarks
of Bloomsbury Publishing Plc

First published in the United States of America 2022

A catalog record for this book is available from the Library of Congress.

ISBN: HB: 978-1-5013-6458-7
PB: 978-1-5013-6457-0
ePDF: 978-1-5013-6460-0
eBook: 978-1-5013-6459-4

Typeset by Deanta Global Publishing Services, Chennai, India

To find out more about our authors and books visit www.bloomsbury.com and
sign up for our newsletters.

Let no one underestimate the strange effect on human psychology of not knowing whether the ground underfoot is ground at all.
　　　　　　　　　　—Helen Macdonald, *Vesper Flights*

Contents

Prologue
No Place Like Home

One spring morning in 2019 I was getting ready for the day when my then eight-year-old son Julien ran into the bathroom. "Papa, someone's ringing the doorbell and pounding on the door!" There was alarm in his voice, and as I left my bedroom I immediately understood why. This wasn't the knocking of a Girl Scout cookie peddler or an Amazon Prime delivery person; it sounded more like what you see on TV shows before a SWAT team bashes down the door.

It was carnival season in New Orleans, which can involve drunken strangers beating on doors where they think there's a party. I was prepared to treat this situation as such an incident. I stumbled downstairs, still wrapped in a towel, and sure enough, a woman's face was in the window, adjacent to the door she was pounding. There was a crazed look in her eyes, and a man standing behind her, in support but just out of the fray. Husband? Brother? Friend? He looked tense, perhaps embarrassed.

"I know my son is in your house! He is a *minor!*" the woman was shouting. "If you don't open up, I am calling the police!"

I didn't know what to do. We had no teenage boy in our house; my son was watching from the top of the stairs and my younger daughter was in her room, obliviously playing. But the woman kept shouting that she had located her son by GPS; she held a smartphone to the window like a search warrant and there, indeed, on an out-of-date satellite view of our block (showing my own house still under construction) you could see a pulsing blue dot located somewhere near the back of our home.

I pieced it together: a phone-tracking app had guided her to my house, and the map on her screen made me guilty of concealing her son—or worse. But when I tried to talk calmly, words were not enough. She brandished her phone. "Why would GPS show him if he's not in there?"

* * *

We'd moved into the house a year before. Before that we had lived in a rickety old shotgun house in a different part of town, nearer to my campus. But with rising costs of living (and two children), we had started a search for a new home, which eventually took us to Mid-City, where the blocks alternated between wastelands and new construction—but where housing prices were far lower. We had imagined getting another old house, but one afternoon we found ourselves on the stoop of a spec house, on a busy street; it was a modern design, by a local architect of some renown, and not at all what we'd had in mind. But our realtor had convinced us that new construction was a smart move—especially in the parts of town prone to flooding. Under the long shadow of Hurricane Katrina and the inevitability of another big storm, buying a house in New Orleans is a risky venture, particularly in the areas that are below sea level. So we walked into the brightly lit, open-floor layout of the new home, and, to our surprise, we loved it.

Walking out onto the back porch during our first visit, I looked out over the matching fenced-in backyards. A cell tower loomed ominously on the near horizon, and electrical mainlines marked an indeterminate barrier in the sky. Amid all the post–Katrina reconstruction, Mid-City stands as a charged space where new buildings and infrastructure are emerging out of the scarred landscape of 300 years of fraught history. A few months later I went to plant a willow sapling in one corner of our yard, and when I dug my shovel through the new sod, what was underneath was barely soil at all. Rather, an eerie amalgam of old wires, broken glass, rusted wrought iron, and ceramic fragments were compacted in a dark clay, remnants of . . . earlier dream houses, perhaps. In this gritty matrix there were no earthworms crawling around—no signs of life.

In that moment when we first looked at the house, I remember thinking it resembled a David Lynch tableau, a perfectly laid-out grid in which something sinister was about to happen (or had already). The real estate pictures had shown an idealized open-floor plan and mid-century modern furniture adorning a domestic interior of the American Dream. But standing outside the actual home, beneath the crackling main electrical lines, it was almost as though something more ominous was going on here. At the time, I wrote this off as a bit of dramatic irony.

*   *   *

In moments like these, your thoughts get loopy. Could her son's phone have ended up on our roof? Or underneath the house? Could he be hiding in our backyard or passed out after last night's parades? Was he dead? Was his body chopped up and packed in a plastic bin in our storage closet? How well do I *really* know my partner?

As the woman grew more frantic, she demanded the names of our family members and our neighbors, and it gradually dawned on me that she *did* seem to have a sense of why her son might be in the neighborhood: a friend's house was in the neighborhood, maybe there had been a clandestine sleepover. She kept repeating *Bourgeois*—a common family name in this region but sounding like a pejorative epithet spat at me as I hid behind the plate glass of my bougie home.

I suddenly recalled that a family a few doors down had a teenager. *Ah, hah!* Could the missing son be at that house? I explained my hunch, and the woman warily backed off the front stoop and marched down the block—glancing back at our door every few steps, as if I might dash out any moment with her boy in a burlap sack.

A few minutes later, as I was getting dressed upstairs, my son hollered up to me that they were walking to their car with a blond-haired teenager in tow. I didn't look, but I pictured him, hanging his head in shame.

*   *   *

The story pretty much ends there.

The phone's locational positioning technology had been off by a few dozen yards. That's it. It's a common experience, when the blue dot on a map app wiggles or strays from where it should be. But usually the stakes aren't so high. It's not typically a missing child, even given our world of horrible headlines of people disappearing, viral stories of bodies showing up in pieces in a gym bag, weeks after having gone missing.

The woman never came back or apologized. We were left feeling rattled and unsettled, a creepy mixture of feelings that lasted all day and into the night. My partner was miffed I had even gone to the door; what if they'd had a gun? I had wanted to defuse the situation—because I "knew" they were mistaken—but she was right: what would another gun murder amount to, in 2019? One data point, lost in a dense skein of political gridlock.

I had been flummoxed by the omniscience of the woman's smartphone app. How could I counter a phone locator app, what the woman repeatedly called "my GPS"? Her certainty of location obliterated what I had taken to be the "reality" of the situation. And while the failure felt profound, I knew it would be easily swept into the dustbin of digital detritus, written off as just another glitch. The omniscience of the machine would be intact; the smartphone would not be held accountable. It would just await another upgrade, refining its search results, homing in on more accurate signals, and continuing doing its work. Or, put another way, we would continue working for *it*.

* * *

Later that morning, I would discuss Edward Said's *Orientalism* with my students. Patches of my face were still flecked with stubble, I had realized, in my office before class; I had been interrupted while shaving. If my students noticed, it wouldn't be the most absent-minded thing I'd ever done in class.

In *Orientalism*, Said wanted to understand how "Arabs" and "Islam" were constructed in the Western imagination, how culture produced a particular and "hegemonic" kind of reality; taking the concept from Antonio Gramsci, Said argued that this "hegemony" is when, for all their freedom of ideas and behavior, individuals find themselves choosing and acting to uphold particular cultural hierarchies, allowing certain forms of life to flourish, over and in place (and to the detriment) of others. "Certain cultural forms predominate over others, just as certain ideas are more influential than others," he writes, but "we can better understand the persistence and the durability of saturating hegemonic systems like culture when we realize their internal constraints [. . .] were *productive*, not unilaterally inhibiting."

Culture doesn't just tell the individual *no*; it tells the individual how to say *yes*. It's a counterintuitive insight, as I tried to explain to my class; what might seem most intact and personal to an individual—their innermost fears and desires—might actually be generated by their culture's "internal constraints." And while the idea of hegemony can sound uncomfortably *Matrix*-y, the sound of that fist on our door was still vivid in my mind, as we talked; I could still see the expression on that woman's face, her anger and certainty. I thought of the smartphone screen she had wielded at me, as *proof* of an unquestionable Truth. If the specter of her missing child had been the source of her passion—and what could be more irreducible than a mother in search of her child?—her phone had been channeling her emotions and dictating her actions.

The more common complaint is that smartphones make us dumber or more passive. But here, the smartphone was dynamically *productive*, producing a real conflict out of a fictional relation: if her son was in my house—and if her smartphone said so, it must be true!—then on what grounds could I close my door to her? What else might I be capable of, and what might she be justified in doing, in response?

*   *   *

When I got home that day, the house felt different. The Lynchian vibe was no longer an imagined campy aesthetic; for a few charged minutes, my home had become the scene of a crime, implicated by the incontestable information of a smartphone. Any minute, another calamity could ensue; all it would take would be for someone's phone to direct them to us. Furthermore, that teen could end up as my student in a couple years.

Home is no longer where the heart is, nor is it based in an analog notion of private property. Home is what is on our phones: home buttons, homepages, home screens. Home is where your GPS tells you it is, what your Uber or Lyft app catalogs as your most commonly used address. Home is changing, and it's not at all clear what it means as it shifts from one digital context to the next. But one thing is certain: in all these productive appropriations and redeployments of the concept, there is no place like home in any simple sense of the word—not these days.

Introduction

The Depressed

When I thought of the title for this book, I figured that it *must* have been done already. It was too obvious: a pun on Paulo Freire's revolutionary treatise *Pedagogy of the Oppressed*, but for now—when so many are so depressed. So I Googled it and was surprised to find that no one else had used this title for a book. (There were some articles that bore the name, but they were somewhat buried away in academic journals.) I had been writing essays about various challenges in the twenty-first-century English classroom, and I figured I could bundle a bunch of them together under this title and make it a timely and maybe even useful book. My editor Haaris Naqvi liked the idea, so I dove in.

I was writing about the insinuation of new technologies in the classroom, from personal smartphones to institutionally adopted learning management systems. I was writing about trigger warnings, increasingly pervasive and layered mental health issues on campus, and how intellectual inquiry was turning into mere data collection. This was all under the darkening shadow of the Trump presidency and on the eroding landscape of higher education across the United States.

But this was before the Covid-19 pandemic, when everything would change so rapidly and all these facets would take on new wrinkles and contortions. So I scrapped the manuscript I had been working with and decided to write this book from scratch, in real time as I taught through the pandemic year of 2020 and as I attempted to find my bearings in this new world. In truth, a lot of things that were nascent before the pandemic just found their way out in the open, as our new normal set in.

I asked a student assistant, Bella Rodriguez-Ramos, to read the early draft of this book—the version I threw away—and after she read it I was relieved to find out that she 'got' the book. Bella understood what I was wrestling with, what I was working through. But she said something that shook me up: she said, "I sort of want you to scream in my face more often." She rightly detected that I was holding something back. So this rewrite of the book is my attempt to speak more directly about what I'm calling *pedagogy of the depressed*. I'm writing it in more of a sprint, to maintain tone and pacing and to track things as they happen. I've reincorporated a few of the original pieces, because they provide critical retrospective moments and punctums.

*   *   *

At a certain point, it seemed like all my students were depressed.

Or, rather, it wasn't a *certain* point at all: it happened "gradually and then suddenly," to borrow a line from Hemingway.

This was depressing. It changed the feel of the classroom, it altered the possibilities of how we could learn together. Students became riddled with depression, anxiety, stress, and other widely diagnosed (or even just *felt*) maladies. And teachers were depressed by this situation, in turn. We were all slogging through the hours, the days, the weeks, the terms, and the years with this crushing sense of . . . something having gone wrong. We were supposed to be at the zenith of higher learning, in a new century with urgent issues to confront and solve. Instead, it felt like each one of us was a little Sisyphus, pushing eternally at our phone screens. And this was all *before* the novel coronavirus arrived.

This isn't a book from the standpoint of psychology or sociology, although I respect these disciplines and draw from some of their vocabulary and perspectives in the following pages. This book, instead, comes at the general topic of depression from the vantage point of the English classroom. I brush against this heavy topic through various encounters with literature, writing, and editing—through practices of working with language, lingering on words, and thinking carefully about written expression. But it's also English with a twist: my own writing and teaching often revolves around air travel, so there's a recurrent theme of flight that appears throughout the book.

My interest in depression here is at least twofold. It's a shared (while also deeply personal) experience among my students, and it's a feeling that I increasingly have when I'm teaching, advising, and mentoring my students. The space of the classroom is also *depressed*: tired, ramshackle, dirty, desks broken, 1.0, passé . . . it's not the space it was just a decade ago. I mean this in a physical sense and also in a medial and cultural sense. The college classroom has become an incredibly vulnerable space, even as we've struggled to try to make it a *safe* space. After Covid-19, it's *really* not the same.

This book is mostly about higher education, but I hope that it might be useful to teachers in a range of educational settings—and even to people at large who find themselves thinking about what lessons to take away from the early decades of the twenty-first century. I wanted to write down some observations, as well as strategies and tactics that I've employed to cope with this general depressed atmosphere of teaching and learning, living and surviving in these times. This is, in short, what I'm calling the *pedagogy of the depressed*.

But if I'm honest, I'm ambivalent about giving advice or offering models. I don't know that effective teaching (much less living) can really be, well, *taught*. I'm not even sure that I've been an effective teacher in these times; oftentimes, at best, I've merely survived. But I have learned some things about coping with the changing landscape of higher education, and I still manage to meet my students each week and we still manage to learn and grow, together.

Then again, I had role models and mentors as I was bumbling into my own teaching career. Of course I *learned* how to be a teacher. (A decent enough one, anyway.) I still sometimes feel as though I am channeling my most inspiring college professors—I can conjure their energy, their commitment, their performances. Yet my pedagogical instincts seem to be failing me, of late. It seems like the classroom has a permanent cloud of sadness—a heaviness—hanging over it. I want to say that this coincided with the election of Donald Trump, but it was no doubt assembling for a while before that gruesome arrival. Still, the toxic name-calling, hellscape news cycle, and frantic media ecosystem ever swirling around Trump did not help things. And the vortex continues each day, as I write this book, even into and through a pandemic that shuttered classrooms everywhere.

When I mentioned on Twitter that I was writing this book, a follower replied, "I'm not sure you're qualified for this, tbh." Twitter being what it is, it was impossible to tell the tone or intent of this reply, but it is something I've wondered myself as I've taken notes, written into, and thought about this topic. Was this person serious or just joking? *Am* I qualified to write about depression? Well, *depression* in what sense?

The "depression" I am interested in tracking in this book is not so much an individual experience, not located (at least not solely) in the depressed *subject*. It's a state of things. It's a depressed atmosphere, a dispersed feeling of dread and weariness that has as much to do with cultural forces and planetary circumstances as it has to do with the intense feeling of solitary helplessness. This definition in the *Oxford English Dictionary* feels accurate to me in its very general sense, its *variousness*:

depression, n.

The action of depressing, or condition of being depressed; a depressed formation; that which is depressed: in various senses (Opposed to *elevation*).

*   *   *

I teach at a small university in New Orleans. It is a diverse and inclusive campus, with many first-generation students and elaborate support systems for students who may need help navigating challenging times and difficult courses throughout their college years. I've taught or guest lectured at a range of other institutions, too, since I started graduate school in 2001. My college-level teaching—for nearly twenty years now—informs this study, the shifts that I'm seeing as well as the hope I still have for a mode of higher education that carries on certain traditions while adapting to the current times of acceleration and exhaustion. What are the signs of these times, specifically? Here are a few snapshots:

A colleague in my department tells me that her students talk about depression almost as an obligatory phase to go through in college. Something they'll just drop, when they graduate. But in the meantime, it becomes something we professors have to reckon with, adjust to. And can it just be "dropped," does it work like that? Depression is sneaky.

Another colleague kills himself, and a shadow of inexplicability hangs over our faculty for years. How was our campus implicated in his suicide, if at all? This was a philosophy professor, very involved in faculty governance and student life. It's hard to believe that conditions around campus were completely apart from whatever pushed him over the edge. But we'll never know.

I am working with a librarian whose job it is to coordinate technology in classrooms, to set up a big display screen in a new seminar room, so instructors can present material for students to interact with. The library tells me "this is an exciting project!"—but this is depressing to me because it (perhaps unconsciously) evinces how pedagogy has become reduced to slick technological potential for projection and display, rather than appreciated for the actual slow, low-tech work that learning together takes. Don't get me wrong: I initiated this, and the librarian was extremely helpful—later that year we awarded her a service award for her incredible work helping the campus adopt new technologies as the pandemic set in. At that point, before Covid, I wanted the ability to show stuff to the class, and so we could collaborate on writing in a live format. But in the moment of planning, it seemed like what was exciting was the technology itself, not what might happen because of it—a less glamorous project indeed.

One friend, a department chair at an R1 university, admits to me over email that he's "spent way more time this fall as chair speaking with faculty who just seem totally beaten down than in previous years." I echoed this sentiment in my reply; I've heard this from countless colleagues at different colleges and universities across the country. And this sense of exhaustion would only expand outward and everywhere, in 2020.

Covid-19 renders classrooms and office hours obsolete, at least for some time—and opening up a floodgate of questions and criticisms about what we've been doing with all this space and time all along. Does higher education really need to take four years? Does it really require traveling somewhere *else*, living there and being with others (in person) and learning together? If we thought higher education was a depressed zone before, what is it in the land of Zoom meetings and the bloom of learning management systems?

This book is an attempt to gather together and clarify my experiences of the changing humanities classroom over the past decade—the humanities classroom and certain cultural vectors that have affected it. My experiences are limited, obviously: to my campus, to my classes, to my region, to my students. But within these constraints, a lot of variation and difference comes through. My intended audience is threefold: college teachers, especially literature and writing instructors; graduate students in the humanities who are facing a rapidly changing cultural landscape; and general readers interested in pedagogy and higher education.

Some of the chapters offer practical, concrete ways that I have coped: in the English classroom, especially, but also in the shifting academic profession at large. I hope these pieces are not didactic or self-congratulatory, but rather may serve as useful prompts for rethinking what it is we do when we teach, when we mentor, and when we learn and create, together—the things that arguably make higher education more important than ever, now. Other chapters are more reflective of general tensions or stressors in higher education. Together, I hope they offer a vivid if impressionistic picture of the pedagogy of the depressed.

I offer this book as a matter of commiseration, solidarity. Out of a sense of desperation, too—unsure, each day, whether I'm doing something that matters or something that is futile in the face of distressing, horrid trends of our species sucking itself into oblivion.

We're All Screens

I never wanted to teach online, because as long as I've believed in college education I have valued the social experience of sitting in a room together—or even better, outside—and learning with and from one another, in person. It doesn't always work. There are uncomfortable silences. People fall asleep or freak out. Sitting together in a room is no guarantee that learning (or anything, really) will happen the way it was planned. But I also think of higher education as a series of time-release capsules and that they differ for everyone in terms of when their efficacy will occur. And so sometimes the most boring or awkward class will yield a lesson much later in life. (This would likely not satisfy administrators who want to be able to assess outcomes directly after a class concludes and grades are filed.)

Teaching at a small liberal arts university as a tenured professor, I had the relative privilege to decide that I wouldn't teach online, even as demand for online courses increased. I taught rather boutique courses, and we had strong enrollments and a popular major. I knew that certain programs offered excellent online courses and degrees. Still, the vexing problem—and opportunity—of online learning was mostly an abstraction, to me. It was something that bothered me, but from a distance.

Then practically overnight in March 2020, teaching online became what everyone was doing. We adapted. I adapted. I used Google Docs for collaborative writing and discussions, and Zoom for group meetings. It helped, at that point, that I'd already gotten to know my students for nearly half the semester. So we could not just focus on keeping the formalities of our classes going but care about one another enough to check in and make sure that we were all surviving. As in, *actually* surviving the novel coronavirus. And helping those infected survive, when they were our family members or friends.

It was a depressing haul, getting through the spring semester trying to keep a modicum of our courses alive. But we did it: the students learned things, reflected on what they'd learned, and even produced final projects. I never wanted to do that again, but it was also clear that online learning had finally claimed its rightful place at the helm of higher education. It wasn't going away, even after the pandemic.

*   *   *

Now I'm teaching practically all online again, the following semester in the autumn of 2020. Most of my students, I've never met in person. Some of them I've only seen once or twice in their Zoom frames, before they endarkened their screens for the duration of the semester. On any given day I might have three or four out of twenty or twenty-five students who enable their cameras; the rest reside behind black boxes. And I can't blame them: this new modality of learning is invasive and encompassing and oppressive in its own right. My colleague and friend Mark Yakich recounted to me how one of our students explained the reason she blacks out her screen: it's that she just needs that minimal separation between her home life and her schooling. I get it. So I talk to a grid of black screens, and students chime in or leave comments in the chat box, and we fumble toward knowledge together. At least, I think that's what we're doing, in our best moments.

And a funny thing has been happening, as I've been teaching mostly online this semester. I'm actually kind of enjoying it. I like preparing my classes each day, assembling some texts to read together or images or video clips to analyze. I don't mind if it's just a few of us having the conversation; I trust that the quiet invisible students are learning by watching and listening. You know why I'm enjoying it, in part? So much of what had become stressful about teaching is suddenly gone.

I had begun to dread one specific part of teaching: having to vie with smartphones for the attention of students—and seeing students tune out one another, in favor of their phones. A lot of professors don't seem bothered by this or seem to tune it out in turn. But it was driving me crazy, when I'd see a student effectively leave class by focusing on their phone, instead. Even if it was just for a second. It could derail my train of thought, or it would especially infuriate me if another student was trying to express a complex idea, in that moment. I'm sure most of the time it wasn't intended to be disrespectful; these things are so baked into our lives by this point that it is almost not worth drawing attention to. Calling out smartphone use in public is gauche, and I am loath to do it. So instead I would seethe as I watched these little handheld screens change the feel of the classroom discussion year by year, more and more.

But now, I *am* the screen. We're *all* screens, as we communicate on Zoom or Google Hangouts. We command attention or black ourselves out if we don't want to be seen doing whatever else it is we're doing during class. All the micromovements and momentarily redirected eyes of classroom phone navigation have been mitigated. Or, rather, it's out in the open in our separate rooms or wherever we are: the privatization promised by smartphones has been cashed out by Covid. Everyone has a room of their own in which to learn, and no one can patrol what screen you're looking at there.

Insanely, the desire to control these things has only increased, in this time. One email sent to the faculty at my university coyly suggested that as we prepared for our next semester's classes, "you may also be thinking about how you will maintain academic integrity in different modalities"—this seemed to be code for an assumption that when learning primarily online, students would inevitably look for ways to cheat. As if to make this paranoia plain, the subject heading of the email was this: "Lockdown Browser & Monitor in 21S Courses." These are apparently software programs available in our learning management system, which respectively "lock a student into a test screen" on their computer and "live record" a student taking a test. Higher education has devolved into a miniature surveillance society!

Not that I will be using any of this dystopian technology. Call me naive, but I still believe in what we're trying to teach our students: *critical thinking*. I've critiqued this phrase before, because it became a meaningless buzzword for so long, but now I find myself rallying around it again. If we hold critical thinking as a skill and as a mindset with which we want to imbue our students, how can we adopt such patently suspicious practices and in the name of *teaching*?

If there's anything liberating or even pleasurable about this now near-universally adopted "modality" of learning—being online together—it's that all the surveilling and monitoring can *go away*. We might trust our students to learn as they can, when they can, without implementing draconian standards or policing mechanisms. I think this is what I am enjoying about teaching online: I don't stress as much about making sure my students are all *on the same page* or paying attention to one another. I let our discussions be even *more* awkward than they were in the physical classroom—and maybe there are new lessons learned through this increased awkwardness, learned by the students who are most engaged and by the students who observe quietly or catch up by reading our class notes, later. Maybe *I* don't have to exert as much control over the paces and styles of their varied paths of learning. (*Especially* in this time of collective existential dread and political tensions stretched to their max, in 2020.)

I've taken a more hands-off approach to teaching, and not because I care less about my students. No, it's precisely because I don't want to be a hassle to them, but want to be available to them as someone who can *help* them—help them learn the material, but also just help them by modeling that we can be in a supportive atmosphere together, and share ideas, and that this does not have to be a high-pressure situation. I don't even grade my students anymore. Instead, I ask them to send me self-reflections midway through the semester, and again at the end of the term, and to supply the grades they want me to enter. This is a very simplified form of "ungrading," which has been justified and promoted by many leading-edge educators of late. It basically empowers students to take more ownership of their educational journeys and to learn to evaluate their own performance and progress, as opposed to being assessed from an as-if objective power above. And it goes well with this new format of teaching, which is—for better or worse—so much more detached and fragmented, compared to the personal, get-to-know-one-another ambience of the traditional classroom.

I find myself balancing this hands-off kind of teaching with an increase in one-on-one mentoring, advising, and helping students work on senior theses and independent studies. Mentoring—really working with students closely—feels more important than ever, in this time of so much online communication. And yet, this too runs into a depressing new reality: the ever-encroaching reign of big data.

Even while writing this chapter, I was scolded by email for not supplying the administration with "early warnings" for my courses. There is an option for reporting "nothing to report"—and reporting nothing to report will satisfy the overseers. But I cannot bring myself to indulge this absurd tautology in the service of depersonalized data harvesting. Wait, let me back up here.

Early Warnings

First come the emails. About three weeks into the semester, the early warning period begins. This is the time when instructors are strongly and regularly urged to submit notices or concerns related to students who may be falling behind or participating irregularly—or, in some cases, who may have disappeared altogether.

The communications come down from the top and are framed with a kind of frantic competitive rhetoric: *Let's see which college will have the highest participation in submitting early warnings! Who will win??? Let's make it 100% participation!*

These messages emanate from the office of the Provost, are forwarded on by the Deans, are circulated through individual departments, and are amplified by the Student Success Center. It's all done with the best intentions, of course. The widely dispersed effort is meant to catch (in the sense of "support") students who really could use help early on to "stay on track"—it's a retention tool, at the granular level.

So what actually happens when a student gets an early warning notification? The student is "caught" in another sense of that term: *support* turns into *surveillance*. This can have unintended consequences. The other thing that comes from early warnings is simply *more emails*. Students are notified by email that they have an early warning. Their academic advisers are then prompted (by email) to follow up with those students—by email. A student who has an early warning in one class may well have early warnings in multiple classes. The student is then potentially faced with a deluge of emails— an uninviting gesture, by any measure.

A problem creeps up here, around the assumption that students know how to manage copious amounts of email—much less *read* them. I'm not faulting students here or saying that they don't know *how* to read emails. I'm simply pointing out that universities often seem to assume that students have already been trained or are naturally able to deal with the flood of emails that comes with college. But this is nothing that an orientation session or email of tips and strategies can easily achieve.

The thing about the early warnings is that the desired outcome is students that are cared for and paid attention to. This is admirable but should go without question. That's what instructors are *for*. This is why advising is *part of my job*. I usually have somewhere between fifteen and twenty-five advisees assigned to me each year. If they stay English majors, I'll work with these students throughout their four years at Loyola, and help them choose their classes and navigate difficulties.

Once every semester, for a two-week period, my advisees can sign up for a one-on-one meeting with me (or sometimes more than one meeting), and we discuss any concerns or questions they have. Sometimes we think through whether they want to add a double major, or a minor . . . or we talk about summer classes, or doing a semester abroad. Advising weeks are intensive and exhausting but incredibly fulfilling: it's where you see the incremental stages and steps of higher education, along the way. It's where you see just how students grow and how their interests develop. Where you see intelligence and maturity in bloom, in process. Advising meetings record an ontography of learning.

But early warnings try to quantify and measure this progress in the crudest way: by interrupting the term, almost right after it has begun, with concern, warnings, and intervention. They are an extension of *helicopter parenting*—but more like *drone* parenting, as these things come unbid and by surprise, initiated as they are by the data-driven offices well beyond the classrooms. It's described as "outreach," but our students may feel it more as *overreach*. I certainly do, as a teacher.

This is all a miserable and depressing replacement for what should be happening anyway in our classes, without the need for bureaucratized monitoring mechanisms: real mentoring. The effort to track and crunch data for early warning submissions also risks turning the actual nuanced practices of mentoring and advising into a matter of mere pushing buttons, box checking, number crunching. There is no "early warning" mechanism that can accurately ascertain the deliberately longer, slower, and sometimes lightning-fast experiences that comprise actual education.

Learning Management

After college, I worked at an airport for a couple years. (I wrote about this experience at length in my book *The End of Airports*.) I was employed by SkyWest Airlines, which was contracted by United Airlines to service the jets that flew into the small airport outside of Bozeman, Montana. This job consisted of two main parts.

First, we were taught the brute outside labor: loading and unloading bags, hooking up the jet bridge, pushing back the plane, de-icing the plane, and so on. All those things you see people in yellow or orange vests doing when you roll up to the gate or before you depart. These myriad tasks were effectively learned on the job. I remember running around beside one of my more experienced coworkers for the first few days, watching and practicing until I could do all these things on my own (and, eventually, train future new hires). Ducking beneath airplane wings; catching roller bags heaved up to me by a coworker; operating the various toggles and switches that made the jet bridge move . . . these were all learned by a quick and close apprenticeship model.

Then there was all the inside work: checking in passengers, issuing tickets, filing lost baggage claims, and making overhead announcements regarding the status of flight. This second type of work required additional training. Specifically, we had to learn the computer reservation system called Apollo, which was a DOS-type program that required two weeks of training at an offsite instruction facility.

My training, in the summer of 2001, took place just south of Seattle in the basement of an office park right near SEA-TAC airport.

SkyWest sent me there on a Horizon/Alaskan Airlines flight and put me up in a nearby hotel within walking distance to the training site. I was given a packet of meal tickets for the cafeteria for breakfast and lunch, as well as a modest cash stipend for dinners.

There were about twelve of us being trained over those two weeks, and looking back, I'm impressed with the pedagogical setup and execution. They were long days in a dark computer lab, but the instructor (I wish I could remember his name; was it Alex? Steve?) was methodical and thorough, pacing us through various exercises as we scaled up our knowledge and skills on the system. There were regular hands-on activities and low-pressure tests to make sure we were absorbing everything. Some became frustrated, but ever-patient Alex/Steve crouched down next to them and helped them troubleshoot and work through problems.

From setting up travel itineraries to booking tickets, from issuing refunds and upgrades to changing routes and dealing with canceled flights, we learned how to satisfy a range of customer needs. The group of students was diverse, having come from all around the Western United States, and spread across a fairly wide age spectrum. Some were like me, young Gen Xers who'd come of age with the internet and had built their own computers in basements, and so could more easily roll with the arcane software; others were Boomers who were still getting used to how computers were rapidly becoming ubiquitous, all but obligatory in everyday life. (Remember, this was 2001.) By the end of the two weeks, we could manage a lot of hypothetical situations and real-world problems. I recall being sometimes bored during, sometimes amused by, but overall *learning* from the relatively intensive training. I made friends with a few of my cohort, and on an afternoon off we took the bus downtown and wandered Pike Place Market, munching smoked salmon strips while gazing out over Puget Sound. This wasn't exactly a paid vacation, but it was the closest thing to it that I'd experienced in my life at twenty-three years old.

That was the thing: these weeks were *fully paid*, and the airline covered the hotel and all meals. I barely had an extra dollar in my checking account at that time, not even a credit card to my name, and so I remember it feeling luxurious: the meal stipend, sitting in an air-conditioned basement learning a skill, venturing downtown in the evenings, having my own hotel room . . . *and being paid for the whole thing!* The airline was clearly investing in us, hoping we'd stay on for a long time. I only worked at the airport for a little over two years, before moving to California to continue my graduate education. But I'll bet that some of my SkyWest coworkers still work for the airline.

The reason I found myself thinking about this time is that my university decided during the 2020 pandemic summer (of all summers!) to switch learning management systems (LMS)—from Blackboard to Canvas (so long Greek mythology, hello obsolete material metaphors). The conversion took place over an already stressful two months, as my exhausted colleagues and I finished our Covid-warped spring semesters and tried to take small breaks or finish lingering projects before the unknown horizon of the Fall was upon us.

Interrupting that break was a tsunami of "implementation updates"—around sixty emails, by my count—frantically trying to get us "up to speed" as we staggered toward the beginning of the term, required to adopt the new software and transition from the old to the new. For many, this meant migrating old classes on Blackboard to the new system, which of course involved various hiccups in formatting, content availability, and accessibility. Many of my colleagues seemed utterly defeated by the task.

Make no mistake: the decision to change LMS platforms was first and foremost a financial one. Canvas, apparently, cut a better deal with my institution and so we dropped Blackboard like dirty PPE. No one really *liked* Blackboard, sure, but I'm not convinced that Canvas

is superior—just different, just a new computer product to become
familiar with and internalize. A virtual contagion of new windows,
tabs, folders, lingo, and buttons to get used to. All while we're trying
to ward off the daily paranoia, information dumps, and continuing
spread of the novel coronavirus.

But here's the thing. Most faculty are on nine- or ten-month
contracts. We're not technically being paid to work in the summers.
(This is why many of us teach summer courses or take on freelance
work: to supplement our salaries.) The administrators and staff who
are aiding the transition from Blackboard to Canvas are being paid
to do that work; they are on twelve-month contracts. And then here
were the flailing instructors who don't yet even know what the fall
semester is *really* going to look like and who were not being paid to
do this preparatory work—much less being paid *extra* to learn a new
computer system, one that was, fundamentally, saving the institution
money.

We're advised to install the Canvas app on our personal
smartphones, so as to best serve our students, but further cutting
into our home lives (whatever that means any more) and requiring
the use of technology and bandwidth that isn't paid for by our
institution.

This distended time has involved so much job spill, multitasking at
new levels, and mental overload. We've had to improvise, cope, make
do, and adjust in every area of ordinary life. These are things we've
become numb to over the past decade—but I felt them more acutely
this summer. In a way, our ever sweeping techno-culture groomed
us for some of these wider effects of the pandemic. While we were
spreading memes and trying to go viral, Covid-19 was preparing to
get into everything and go everywhere. All our work was about to
bleed into everything else—or become stanched.

No one asked for this, and no one knows when (or how) it will
end. Our overlapping frameworks of lockdown, quarantine, isolation;

homeschool, un-school, canceled summer activities; home office, no office; Zoom meetings, FaceTime, advertisements for masks ad nauseam . . .

In some ways it was just absurd to the point of being laughable that the switch from Blackboard to Canvas had to happen this summer. In other ways it's soul crushing, one more insult added to widespread injury.

I think back on my two weeks in Seattle, being paid to learn the Apollo reservation system for United Airlines. This time was bracketed, reserved for learning—and entirely paid for by the company. Compare that relatively quaint time with the frenzied 2020 summer of email blasts, ad hoc training sessions, and mandatory conversion foisted upon by my university—all to squeeze some thousands of dollars so as to protect the highest salaried administrators, as well as the university's endowment.

Of course, airlines and academia were both in crisis mode during this time.

Despite my somewhat nostalgic recollection of the United reservation system training, airlines are by no means innocent entities; labor unions exist for good reason. I can also recount some horror stories from my time working at the airport. Airlines have benefited greatly from the CARES Act, and as I write this the airlines are also frantically trying to ramp up business again. As a recent *Wall Street Journal* article headline quoted the CEO of American Airlines, "Let's Go Fly, for God's Sake." Even when to "go fly" is no isolated act: air travel is clearly implicated in the ongoing second surge of Covid cases.

My Apollo training exists in something of a time capsule, anyway, before smartphones and other burgeoning technologies so radically changed (and merged) the landscapes of work and everyday life. The uncomfortable truth is that all the things we're feeling so powerfully now have been in the works for some time. The novel coronavirus is inextricably an extension of our species—a new but also momentary outcome of the Anthropocene, or humans' ability to spread and move around so efficiently around the planet. This is our job, what we've been trained to do. Whether we will continue to do this work, or change, is another matter. One that my students, perhaps, will have a better sense of than the failing generations ahead of them did.

4

Against Sheep

I was shopping for groceries in my neighborhood market. Everyone was wearing masks and giving each other plenty of space. People were being respectful, and if you paid attention, you could decipher the creases around eyes when we smiled at one another from behind our masks. It was a model day of civility in the midst of the pandemic.

But as I turned into the condiment and sauces aisle, I noticed a shopper whose mask wasn't fully on. Actually, it could scarcely be called a "mask"—it barely covered her mouth and looked more symbolic than functional. And it was a strange symbol: scrawled across the filthy white fabric in red all-caps was the word *SHEEP*.

I was struck by this effort to combine minimal compliance with defiant counter-messaging. Was she trying to shame the wearers of facemasks, by calling us sheep? As in, we were all behaving like a flock, following orders mindlessly? And doing this precisely *on* her own non-mask, to make the point all the more bitter? What were we supposed to do with this act of non-simple rebellion? Become suddenly awakened, like Neo in *The Matrix*? Or get angry, start a scuffle? Initiate a conversation? I zoned out while staring at the jars of small pickles, as I considered my fellow consumer. Was I just a sheep, wearing my custom-made little mask and standing here fogging up my glasses? Even if so—weren't we all just sheep, milling about in this grocery story, anyway?

As I continued my shopping I saw her a couple more times—ambling along like the rest of us, filling her cart, looking for deals. I kept waiting for someone to confront her—*Cover your nose, please!*—

but no one did. Maybe we'd reached a state of shared exhaustion, when it comes to trying to convince people that public health matters. Maybe we'd just become resigned to the slow burn of ideological gridlock defining our age.

A day later I went to my university campus, for the first time since the coronavirus forced us all online back in the spring. A few students were heading to their Hybrid/HyFlex classes, all wearing masks, walking well apart from one another. Ample signage explained what doors to use and how to give appropriate space to others. Out on the quad, spry little signs were stuck in the lawn, channeling our school mascot, Havoc T. Wolf. One sign read: "A HEALTHY PACK STARTS WITH YOU"—and under that, "MASKING MEANS CARING FOR YOUR WHOLE SELF AND WHOLE COMMUNITY." A cartoonish wolf wore a mask on all these signs: piercing blue eyes still fierce, but no teeth bared.

These signs displayed a fascinating negotiation, conjuring the individualist spirit of the lone wolf and then yoking it to a collective impetus to maintain a common good. But it's easy enough when the animal of motivation is a *leader*. The mythology of wolves is agreeable precisely because it keeps intact the centrality of the individual: a healthy pack *starts* with you. But is this in fact correct, biologically speaking? No. A healthy pack, whatever that is, always depends on myriad factors and other entities that lie outside of the lone wolf and indeed beyond the pack itself. A healthy pack doesn't really "start" with anything at all but is a fragile and temporary result of an elaborate, ongoing interplay.

I appreciated my university's attempt to get everyone to mask up. The Jesuit ideal of *cura personalis*, or care for the whole self, was neatly extrapolated for the sake of the "whole community." But the wolf metaphor bugged me, in this context. I guess it's okay to be a wolf, leading a pack—but not a sheep, following one's flock? Why is it okay to laud certain animals and disparage others? What do we want from animal metaphors? To carry some things over and leave others behind.

*   *   *

My son's tenth birthday was in July of the pandemic summer. We invited my parents, and my siblings and their children, to meet in a nearby meadow for a social distanced party, with masks. Given our location, on the edge of a national lakeshore, pretty far from the nearest town, it may have seemed like overkill. We had all been relatively isolated for some time, at that point, and none of us worked in a public place. But still, we wanted to be safe; and my sisters and I felt like it was important to model mask wearing for our children—to normalize it, for the uncertain duration.

My father wrote an email reply explaining that he would stay home that day, since he believed masks were "worthless." No matter that the scientific consensus was in, by then: masks really did make a difference when it came to tamping down the spread of the virus. For whatever reason, this was a sticking point with him—wearing a mask was something he wouldn't do, even for the sake of his grandson's birthday, even for a couple hours. He hadn't worn a mask since the spread of the coronavirus began, and he wasn't about to. He was a skeptic. Yet there was an underlying irony to my father's refusal to don a mask: he had been sick with a range of suspicious symptoms for the previous two weeks and had attempted to get a Covid test but was flustered by the long wait times and circuitous scheduling protocols. He seemed to be recovering by the time of the party, but my siblings and I were being reasonably cautious.

Looking back, I suspect there was something in my father's mindset akin to that of the *SHEEP*-mask wearer. Wearing masks was a sign of weakness—an admission of base animality. Admitting the severity of the virus was similar: an acknowledgement of vulnerability, that we were just creatures whose biological systems could be compromised.

To wear a mask to a grandson's birthday party would be to concede that there were things out of our control. That we were mere beings, among other beings coalescing and competing for a brief stint at life.

But then, my father was comfortable speculating about "herd immunity" as a desirable achievement. Wasn't this, though, an animal figuration as well? I suppose that a *herd* sounds strong—dominating, even. Picture the herd roving across a fecund valley: vibrant life. It's not so unlike the wolf, a natural born leader—even in a mask. It hinges on the creature and how aspirational the fantasy world is that comes with it. Some animals we apparently want to emulate or admire. But sheep, they are just waiting to be decimated by a shrewd predator . . . or led by a god. Ambivalence runs strong here, like a river choked with salmon fighting the current.

*   *   *

In a passage of his journal from March 31, 1842, Henry David Thoreau pondered some unlikely affinities between humans and fish:

> How many young finny contemporaries of various character and destiny, form and habits, we have even in this water! And it will not be forgotten by some memory that we *were* contemporaries. It is of *some* import. We shall be some time friends, I trust, and know each other better. Distrust is too prevalent now. We are so much alike! have so many faculties in common! I have not yet met with any philosopher who could, in a quite conclusive, undoubtful way, show me *the*, and, if not *the*, then how *any*, difference between man and a fish. We are so much alike! How much could a really tolerant, patient, humane, and truly great and natural man make of them, if he should try? For they are to be understood, surely, as all things else, by no other method than that of sympathy. It is easy to say what they are not to us, *i.e.*, what we are not to them; but what we might and ought to be is another affair.

We are so much alike! The repetition of that claim is arresting. Humans and fish. Are we really more alike than different? Of all creatures to make this comparison: *fish*? I've spent a lot of my life among fish, wading in their waters and attempting to catch them, if only to release them back in their element. And I have to admit that it's the profound *differences* between me and them—and between different species *of* fish—that attract me to lingering among them. But I think I get what Thoreau is saying, on some level: we share with fish so many of the drives and instincts that cause us to move and to commingle on our shared planet. Many fishes swim in schools; and we humans thrive in groups, as well—though we often try to repress this fact.

But Thoreau's reflections aren't just about humans and *fish*. The impulse here is about seeking out commonality—and having sympathy for others. Sympathy. It's more popular today to talk about empathy. So why does Thoreau suggest *sympathy*? For one thing, *empathy* wasn't in English usage when Thoreau was writing—it would only appear in the language more than fifty years later. Whereas empathy has come to connote a fairly narrow meaning—feeling for someone else while acknowledging one's own distance from the subject's particular position—sympathy is a more capacious term and perhaps more useful for undoing the knots of animal metaphors pulled so tight around facemasks during our pandemic. Sympathy is more a confused comportment: it variously suggests sharing feelings, having sensitivity for and with others, perceiving relationships, and realizing unity across difference.

The thing about pejorative animal metaphors is that they are *speciesist*: they are implicitly an assertion that some species are less valuable or advanced than others. This may seem innocuous, or merely descriptive. One could imagine the *SHEEP*-mask wearer saying something like, "I'm not *against* sheep, but just pointing out that people are *acting* like sheep." But the dig is clear; sheep are lesser beings. And another assumption creeps in here: humans are obviously the *best* beings.

So much depends on an assumed premise of human superiority. It may seem natural or inevitable to believe one's species to be primary and/or at the pinnacle of an evolutionary process (even though evolution is *not* linear).

But the trouble with speciesism is that it often contains, nestled within—or can so easily become—*racism*. If it seems effortless to prioritize one species over others, it's not much of a step to do the same within arbitrary divisions of a species itself. It all comes back to the primacy of the self. No, it's stronger than primacy—it's unflinching superiority. When it is acceptable to say that certain species are valuable or admirable and others worthless or disposable, this same logic can be transposed onto how people treat one another. Humans have historically treated race as an as-if natural marker of separation, one that imbues perceived difference with forces of opposition and domination. This is the history of violence maintained by racism: groups of people demarcated in order to be subjugated, murdered, enslaved, transported against their will.

Here was my epiphany, as I thought more about the *SHEEP*-mask: This is why the nexus of protests against racial injustice and the Covid-19 pandemic is no coincidence. In both cases, large collectives are at stake—and this makes some people very uncomfortable, because their sense of innate superiority is being challenged. Imagine what a real collective reckoning with the pasts of slavery and settler colonialism in the Americas could look like. If reparations and reconciliation were not up for debate, but were a long overdue given. If it were inconceivable to object on any grounds, because, well, this is what *happened.*

Now imagine if humans had, early on in the spread of the novel coronavirus, perceived the virus not as an evil other to be vanquished but—bear with me—as a sort of kin and with *sympathy*. What if instead of seeing an infiltrating entity with which to do battle, we would have seen the virus as a "contemporary," to use Thoreau's word. Indeed, the virus was able to travel so efficiently and effectively throughout human populations precisely because we served both as a model and medium. Our airplanes were their airplanes; our gatherings, their gatherings. We have been companion species in this pandemic. Now, if the shared goal became to slow the spread of the virus, so to better understand and live *with* the virus, we might have changed our collective patterns for some time—really changed them, not just grumpily put up with lockdowns for a few weeks or months. We might have recognized the virus as unique and yet similar to us, and—respected it.

I'll admit that this is a big leap, perhaps too big for us. And I don't mean to gloss over the innumerable structural and systemic problems that are vitally important to remedy, as well. But understanding that this will most likely not be the last pandemic we see in the coming years, it is worth considering our underlying mentalities and reactions. To usher in a significant transformation on the societal and even global level, these need to be radically adjusted.

I'm not against sheep. But neither am I overly *for* wolves. Fish aren't the best species; viruses aren't the worst. And humans are right there in the mix. What would it take to amplify this message, to work toward more patience and sympathy, across and embracing differences? The lesson here is to be attentive to animal metaphors. All metaphors, really—but animal ones in particular. Because they are us.

*   *   *

Halfway through the fall semester, I was preparing to return to campus to teach in-person again, for the first time in eight months—since the coronavirus landed in New Orleans. I was giddy with excitement. I had the sense that students—at least some students—were eager to be together again and to be with me (many who I'd never met in person, yet). I think they wanted a *person* teaching them. Even, maybe, a *persona*. A character to act out this part of their lives, their teacher in college. But I might be reading too much into it—I might have been projecting my own giddiness onto them.

Would it be weird, or uncomfortable, teaching with a mask? I didn't even consider it—perhaps because by that point masks had become normal and everywhere. On people's faces, discarded on the sidewalks and choking the gutters all around town. We'd be outside, anyway—sitting in a wide circle, on the grass. My only dilemma was this: print out texts for my students, or would they recoil at this old-world, germ-spreading tradition? I decided to just print a few pages and lay them in the sun for a while before class—and I'd inform them of my safety measures before setting them in the middle of our circle, where students who wanted them could venture in and take one. (I'd emailed my students the texts, anyway, so they could read them on their phones or laptops, if they preferred.)

But then came the night before class. I woke up paranoid, wondering if I was being needlessly reckless. What was so wrong with Zoom? Did we really *need* to meet in person? Was I rushing it?

The first thing I had to do in the morning was to fill out a "campus clear" form, confirming that I had no symptoms and that I hadn't tested positive for Covid-19. This protocol seems mostly harmless, and it's an effective way to encourage self-monitoring within a community, during the pandemic. (Of course, it also further normalizes ubiquitous technologies of surveillance, but that's an argument for another time.)

Seven students out of twenty-three showed up, and we sat in a wide circle—but no wider than usual, really, with so few present. My students and I discussed realism and how texts can use and warp realism, to different ends. In our masks, spaced out like that, we learned—and we were humbled. Campus was hauntingly quiet. Only a few students walked by during class, and I didn't see groups of administrators on their way to meetings. Our meeting felt all the more special, for being so anomalous.

Wearing masks was fine; they were a regular garment feature of our lives by this time. Crows flew by, angling down over the quad and soaring up into tree limbs at the last moment. Anole lizards skittered up and down the sides of buildings. Ants marched along in continuous lines at the edge of the lawn. *We are so much alike!* Yet we didn't feel like sheep. Or wolves, for that matter. We just felt like humans, pantomiming a college class.

Sitting six feet apart from one another didn't seem awkward. The one thing I did notice was that it was harder for my jokes to land; or at least, I couldn't tell if and when my students laughed. This caused me to wonder: Does too much of my pedagogy rely on humor, even sometimes shock comedy? Is this my way of dealing with the heavy cloud cover of depression over campus, over the world?

Our seventy-five minutes passed quickly. I felt energized from the experience—it had felt like forever since I'd taught a class like that, in-person. But then, after I got home, an email from a student who had been there, sitting across from me on the grass, so peacefully and attentively:

I have been in close contact with someone who has tested positive for Covid-19. I will not be able to attend in-person classes until October 15th at the earliest, but I will know more information after I get tested this weekend.

The pandemic strikes back.

I met my students again a few weeks later—three of them, next time—and we sat in the quad spaced out again and in our masks, and we discussed a Claudia Rankine essay on white male privilege at the airport ("liminal spaces i" from *Just Us*). It was a lot of work, the four of us close reading passages and transcribing notes online in real time, for our classmates who weren't able to join us. The uncertainty of the imminent election hung in the air, as did the latest spike in coronavirus cases. But, we were also—almost—getting used to this.

5

Trigger U.

Rewind to September 2019: "Hey Papa, we had a lockdown drill at school today."

My son tells me this after school, and my five-year-old daughter quickly corroborates it: "Yeah, we all had to go into the bathroom! It was stinky!"

They were told, apparently, that it was a *drill*. But I know, thanks to the alert message texted to me by the school, that in fact it wasn't a drill. There was an unidentified person in the school building—someone who turned out to be a caterer bringing food, but for an uncertain ten minutes or so, it was cause for a lockdown.

It could have become an active shooter situation.

* * *

I remember racing down empty cornfield roads in southern Michigan with my English professor Pete Olson one mild April afternoon in 1999. On the radio, we were listening to the news of the Columbine school shooting as reports came in. Pete was from Colorado originally, knew the place well—so he was tuned in to the details. We were on our way to pick Pete's two daughters up from school. I babysat them occasionally and was close to both; I could tell Pete was anxious to get the girls.

Six months later, our college president's daughter-in-law, who worked in public relations and marketing for the school, committed suicide in a gazebo on the campus arboretum—using a firearm from the family's gun locker. The scandal that unfolded in the aftermath exposed deep hypocrisy within the college's leadership, and the events left students reeling in confusion and, in some cases, trauma: the scene of the suicide had been visible from one of the women's dormitories, and the student support staff was ill-equipped to help students process what they had witnessed.

*   *   *

A dozen years after all this, I had the good fortune of meeting at a conference Sarah Allison, a Victorianist and Digital Humanities scholar who now teaches alongside me in my English department. What I didn't know until a couple years after we began working together was that Sarah was a senior at Columbine the year of the infamous mass shooting. Sarah has been working through this subject in her own writing, and I've benefited from thinking about the complexities around and within trauma, storytelling, and healing, thanks to her camaraderie.

It struck me at a certain point that my own educational and pedagogical paths were also punctuated by school shootings, directly and indirectly. I was living with this particular form of trauma at the periphery of my thought, the possibility of a shooting always vaguely in mind as I taught and learned with my students.

*   *   *

Lucy Corin's story "My Favorite Dentist" is set during the time of the Washington, D.C. sniper attacks of October 2002. The characters go about their days with an understated awareness of a lurking sniper and the suspenseful possibilities of being suddenly shot at. Driving home after a dentist appointment, the narrator describes how "Home is not far but it takes a long time with all the lights. Also, because of the sniper, a lot of people are trying to drive with their heads ducked." It's just another day in the early twenty-first century, where gun violence has been rendered into talking points and practical factoids.

Later in the story, the narrator's neighbor Andrea waves from her screened-in porch: "Hey, can you come over? Hey, did you hear they want us to walk zigzag? You going in or you coming over? Decide or get down quick while you think, girl." The narrator responds, "There aren't any sidewalks. . . . What are we supposed to zigzag *on?*" To which Andrea replies, "I walked zigzag from the Rite-Aid to my car, in and out. Are you coming?"

Corin's suburban tale is perforated by the present absence of "the sniper," a murky figure who threatens to appear. But the narrative is enveloped by an atmosphere of exhaustion, in which the characters seem to barely have room to fit this new threat into their already crowded, consumerist, and anxious everyday lives.

I remember when I taught "My Favorite Dentist" in an American Fiction course in 2010 at Loyola University New Orleans, how the conversation quickly turned to survival tactics. One of my students was from the D.C. area and remembered her family taking similar precautions to the ones described in Corin's short story. Other students talked about being robbed by gunpoint around New Orleans—with tips about places to avoid at night—or recalled the heavily armed squads that patrolled the streets of the city post-Katrina.

Looking back on that class, I realize I probably could have given a trigger warning for the content of the story, particularly for students who had experienced gun violence or the ambient threat thereof. But then, maybe we had all been triggered already by that point. We'd been growing accustomed to active shooter events and now just seeing them reflected in the annals of contemporary fiction. For a couple years, our university had an ad that ran on the side of the streetcars as they trundled throughout town: "The World Is Our Blackboard." But what a world this was! Maybe all colleges around the country were becoming something else, if unknowingly: *Trigger U.*

* * *

Up until the pandemic, school shootings had become terrifyingly common events. Or if not *common*, at least legible: they fit readily into an available topology of headlines, narratives, and responses. Their potential for occurrence has been almost normalized, resulting in active shooter drills (or actual protocols) such as my children have experienced. I remember seeing a macabre joke online after the initial lockdown orders went into place, something to the effect of *Well at least I don't have to worry about my kid getting shot at school, now.*

On my university's website, I can watch a training video called "surviving an active shooter event." I can download and print a Department of Homeland Security "Active Shooter Pocket Card." This jam-packed informational document tells me in laughably miniscule print all I need to know, including a concise definition: "An active shooter is an individual actively engaged in killing or attempting to kill people in a confined and populated area, typically through the use of firearms." Easy enough!

This ambience of preparedness can tend to breed paranoia. My colleague Mark Yakich has been doing research into bulletproof backpacks; he plans to purchase one using his endowed professorship funds, since such armor has technically, in a way, become part of the job. Unfortunately, Mark has learned that these backpacks often won't do more than stop a single small-caliber pistol bullet, while the reality of active shooter situations is often more dire, involving assault rifles or other semiautomatic weapons.

Even when Mark found a candidate that would seem to do the job—the Guardian 1—and he told me all about it, I had the uncanny feeling that we were being interpellated into the very nightmare we were hoping to avoid. The advertising copy at Amazon.com went into exhaustive detail—a swift education in active shooter theory, as it were: "Threat Level III rated anti-ballistic material is resistant to 7.62mm FMJ lead core rifle ammunition, as well as to most handgun ammunition including .22SR, .22LR .25, .32, .38, .380, .357Magnum, 9mm Full Metal Jacket, .40 Cal., .45cal., and .44 Magnum." And there are caveats: "Threats from unusual high-velocity ammunition, armor piercing ammunition, sharp-edged or pointed instruments and other unusual ammunition or situations may defeat bulletproof products. Also, at some angles, projectiles can slide or deflect off the edges of the bulletproof panels or ricochet." *At some angles*: all those trajectories that can never be controlled or planned for, the very condition of mortal existence.

Elsewhere on the product page, a punchy tagline appears: "Have fun. Be safe. Life is precious." What a curious triumvirate of axioms; in any one of my literature classes, we would rip it to shreds. But, as such, it's hard to argue with the persuasive rhetoric of this bulletproof pack.

How did we come to this, introspective English professors frantically Googling body armor as part of our daily activities?

It's not just us. It's in the air. Or rather, it's on our campus.

* * *

On November 4, 2019, an email was sent from our university's administration, informing everyone that there would be filming taking place on campus later that week:

> The storyline calls for an actor to run around with a fake gun scaring the background actors. Many, if not all of the participants will be dressed in military gear. There may be shouting or screaming, but there will not be any gun sound effects. . . . Signs will be clearly posted marking the filming location, and NCIS security and LUPD will be on hand to reassure onlookers that the activity is staged and that the gun is made of rubber.

NCIS is a crime drama that on any given day is snarling the residential streets and urban lanes around New Orleans with its production trucks, lighting equipment, personnel vans, and so on. Most of the time I just tune it out; it's a vague annoyance but one that quickly recedes in the rearview mirror.

But the announcement of this campus intrusion was alarming—particularly given coincident efforts at our university to support students who are experiencing anxiety, depression, post-traumatic effects, and other real if sometimes delicate obstacles that get in the way of their educational paths.

The email was intended, I gathered, to be a kind of trigger warning: a flag that what was coming could be troubling to people on campus, and so they could choose to opt out. In this case, though, the campuswide email was profoundly strange: it was a trigger warning for, well, a *trigger*—as a synecdoche for *gun*. Trigger warning: in a few days, there will be a gun being waved around campus and people running away from the (fake) shooter, and screaming.

By alerting us that there would be staged violence on campus, for the sake of filming, the specter of an active shooter situation was inevitably raised. The message insisted that the gun would be fake, indeed that it was "made of rubber"—though the latter point came across as an absurd obfuscation, insinuating that the weapon in question would be almost bright-colored and jiggly, when we know very well that guns on TV are absolutely realistic, no matter what they are "made of." Furthermore, the mention of the LUPD (the campus police) being on hand in fact assured us that there would be *real* guns in the mix, as well.

The email ended with an awkward sort of apology for this whole spectacle. The subtext, of course, is that we needed the money. Our university has been on hard times, financially speaking, and most likely charges a decent fee for the use of our campus. But given our university's commitment to social justice and sensitivity to the psychological well-being of our students, the business of being a "backdrop for scary scenes" risked ringing a bit tone-deaf. The email closed with the positive message that this film appearance would let "our campus shine in the spotlight"—yet given the backdrop, this had the mood of floodlights after a calamity more than an occasion for pride and prestige.

Behind the ham-fisted email, the bottom line was that the administration had agreed to let NCIS film a shooting scene on our campus. And no matter how much intellectual distance from, no matter the amount of explanation of the simulation in advance, the fact of the matter is that the campus would resemble and enact an active shooter situation—all to make a quick buck.

I was rattled by the email. I was worried for my students who might actually be triggered by this scenario, and I was eager to talk it over with Sarah Allison, too. Was there something we should do, as faculty? Could this bungled messaging have been avoided, somehow? Was this for-profit staging of our campus as a site for an active shooter event in line with our university's mission to "work for a more just world"?

The worst part was that when I brought it up with my students the next day, no one had even read the message. They are so inundated these days with mostly meaningless emails from myriad sources, and another announcement from the university didn't even get their attention.

When I told my students about the imminent filming, and the armed-gunman-chase-scene in store, many were outraged. A few just shrugged or wanted to go check out the production setup after class.

On the day of the filming, my historian colleague Justin Nystrom tweeted, "Somehow having a tv show film a fake shooting scene outside my office is screwing with me. Was it being at Virginia Tech in 2007? Oh right, right. It is that."

A short video shot from Justin's office window showed people running and screaming across the quad: choreographed pandemonium, but still eerily real, given that this is the actual place where we teach and mingle every day. This scene was taking place on the literal ground where I like to hold my classes. I hadn't realized that Justin, too, carried the traces of a campus shooting in his past: he was a student at Virginia Tech when the shooting happened. I

wondered how many of *our* students had had active shooters on their
high school campuses or trauma from encounters with other "scary
scenes" that the *NCIS* menagerie might uncomfortably recall.

Some students reported hearing gunshots, even though we had
been told there wouldn't be any. There was mild outrage on Twitter
and in a few hallways on campus, and then the incident faded from
conversations as the *NCIS* crew dismantled their set and were gone,
onto film another scene, somewhere else in town. So audiences could,
later, watch the chase scenes and shootings from the comfort of their
couches at home.

Conceivably, there are certain themes or settings that the university
wouldn't have been okay with, even in simulacral form, even for the
highest fee. Like an abortion clinic depicted on our campus or maybe
a scene in which sacred religious texts were destroyed in plain sight.
But an active shooting event was, apparently, considered fair game—
secure in the land of fiction, obviously fake. Even if it could happen
for real, tomorrow.

The United States amasses more guns each year per capita than any
other country in the world, and sociopolitical tensions are running
at an all-time high. Potential shooters know that they will have an
audience, that this form of expression is newsworthy and perfect for
social media. The truth is that the possibility of a real active shooter
event is increasingly nearby, always right around the corner, if not also
in one's not-too-distant past, or on nightly TV. Trigger U. Coming to
a campus near you.

6

Ecophobia

Allergies are one thing; if any student has allergies, we stay inside—no debate. But once the lingering summer boil finally releases its hold, autumn in New Orleans is usually quite pleasant for sitting outside and discussing literature and ideas. It's been harder than usual, though, to coax my students to hold class outside.

I'm talking about discomfort with the physical world outside our campus buildings, things like sitting on grass: many students just won't do it. They might stand, or we've sometimes situated our oval seminar shape so that half of them sat on a sidewalk, while the rest of us sat on grass. With a grungy aesthetic very much the mode on my campus, I don't think it's about keeping their J.Crew slacks unblemished. (It seems like everyone's wearing mom jeans, these days.) And I'm not saying that the grass-sitters are morally superior.

We're reading Virginia Woolf's genre-defying *Orlando* in my class this semester. Nature plays a strange role in this text, as something that the eponymous character worships but which patently resists being written about. At one point early in the book, this problem is made plain: "Nature and letters seem to have a natural antipathy; bring them together and they tear each other to pieces." Part of this book is about Orlando's prolonged struggle to complete a poem called "The Oak Tree." The poem is based on a real oak tree near Orlando's childhood home, beneath which Orlando likes to sit and think. My students think I'm making a little joke when we sit beneath a maple tree on our campus to talk about *Orlando*. (It's really just for shade.) We were in the midst of discussing a particular scene—one of Orlando's "Jay

Gatsby" phases, as a student rightly described it—when I saw a couple students guffawing at the tree trunk behind me. I asked what they were looking at, and one exclaimed, "There are *hella* lizards on that tree!" Sure enough, there were brown anoles all over the bark, chasing each other around and displaying their signature dewlaps. By some accounts, a population explosion has led to these invasive reptiles being far more visibly present around New Orleans in recent years.

About ten minutes after the brown anole incident, another student shrieked and jumped up as an insect arced over her leg. "*It's a cicada!*" The two students next to her scattered, and a fourth stood up and promptly stomped on the critter as it trundled across the sidewalk. Several of their classmates gasped in horror; one or two cheered. It hadn't looked like a cicada to me: when I went over to examine the remains, I found it was in fact a chubby mole cricket, a kind we rarely see because they burrow. It was twitching with its last efforts at life.

I couldn't tell if the student who had killed it felt guilty or proud, or a bit of both. But it took us a few minutes to get back on track. In a bizarre coincidence, we landed on a page where we learn that Orlando "could not endure to see a donkey beaten or a kitten drowned." What about mole crickets squashed?

There are innumerable distractions when teaching a class outside. Friends ambling across campus, ongoing maintenance projects around the quad, cute service animals accompanying fellow students, National Air Guard F-15s screaming overhead practicing for urban warfare. . . . But in my experience, this cacophony also makes class more immediate. We really have to *work* to pay attention, to follow a thread, to articulate a point. We have to read passages out loud clearly and with more intensity—to make them heard over the sounds of lawn care equipment whining or crows cawing in the palm trees. But when the students can't stop obsessing about the ants beneath them—not the biting fire ants, just normal little black ants—or even bear to repose on the ground, class gets extra challenging.

My colleague Hillary Eklund, who also works on environmental themes in literature and culture, corroborated my experience, when I shared my flustered state with her after class: she'd had a stander in an outside class, too, and said her students were generally not happy about being outside.

"What is going on?" I asked.

"It's *ecophobia*."

In his book on the subject, Simon Estok defines the term "ecophobia" as "a uniquely human psychological condition that prompts antipathy toward nature." If our students are more ecophobic than they've been in the past, this is curious. For one thing, they're more aware than ever of climate change and rising sea levels, not to mention our own disappearing coast. Why would they be so scared of what's right outside the classroom?

Strolling across campus one afternoon, I watched as a student in front of me glared up at the sun, which was preventing him from reading his smartphone. It was an odd moment, as if he was completely annoyed at this obtrusive *thing* in the sky—this remote yet warm orb that makes our lives on this planet possible in the first place.

Today's college students have lived much of their lives with smartphones, and I think this is one of the latent causes of ecophobia. On the smartphone, everything is contained, curated, compartmentalized—even news of environmental catastrophe. Furthermore, smartphones function best inside. (That's where the power is, too.) Sure, we use smartphones everywhere we go, inside and outside. But their natural habitat, so to speak, is a climate-controlled, light-controlled interior—preferably near an outlet.

Being outside for a sustained period—seventy-five minutes, in our case—might be scary in part because it's harder to use a phone as effortlessly as we've become accustomed to. Without desks in front of everyone, it's harder to conceal a smartphone use during class. That pesky sun gets in the way. And then, all the other creatures and features of our extended biome start making their presence known. If smartphones work hard to produce a feeling of a whole world in one's palm, *pace* Blake, the outside world disrupts this feeling in subtle and not so subtle ways. Ecophobia, then, might be a natural response to the low-grade anxiety of one's smartphone being put in its place—or rather, put out of its place.

There was one class last spring that subverted this trend. I had just handed out a poem from that week's *New Yorker*, "April," by Sandra Simonds. The poem begins, "The red bird falls from the tree, lands on / its head. Rolls / right back onto its feet. Hello spring. / Hello, sanity. Hello, trashfire century."

We were sitting in a courtyard outside the music building, and as we settled in and started to discuss the poem that I'd handed out, we heard a faint thump against a window above us. A sparrow hit the ground within a few feet of our class circle. We watched its thin tarsus and delicate toes rigidify as it died; its eyes clouded into a matte black. My students were flabbergasted; the moment was uncanny, to say the least. It was one of those teaching moments that I live for. When everything converges, and learning and real life are suddenly exposed as one and the same. There we were reading a poem about precarious life and current anxieties, when BAM. Objective correlative.

One student was particularly distraught by the incident, and after class a few of us moved the dead bird off the concrete slab and to the base of a nearby tree, where we built a small tomb out of twigs. We assured one another that the bird would be better recycled into the circle of life, here.

This day galvanized our class in a funny way. It was as if after that serendipitous crash, my students realized that literature isn't just about ideas or florid language but about the real world we all live in and depend on for survival. How to create these opportune moments not just outside but in the classroom as well, so as to instruct and inspire my students?

Of course the inside/outside binary doesn't hold up with even the most cursory ecological perspective. These buildings, these phones, even these "letters" (to use Woolf's word) are part of our *extended phenotype*. We are another species doing its thing on this planet, for better and for worse. There is no getting outside of nature—this is it, all of it.

And my students make connections that I could never anticipate. Like when I received an excited weekend email from one student this semester with the subject line "Orlando is EVERYWHERE," alerting me to an online article about how the MET Gala theme was inspired by *Orlando*. My students are engaged in ways I can't fully understand, and they know far more about the burgeoning world than I do; the limits I fear may just be my own limits.

So the truth is that I may be suffering from my own form of ecophobia. If I'm honest, I have to say that I don't know how to handle the influx of phones in the classroom, or the rapidly changing dynamic on college campuses due to the normalized option (or even preferred mode) of online education, which is altering long-held realities of traditional university life. Airplanes increasingly unsettle me, not just thundering across the sky but as speculative or grounded metonymies of the Anthropocene, as well. What might they transport, next? *I'm* freaked out about the world, in its present state. My students and I are in this together: working to live in and learn from this world, even with trepidation.

7

Environmental Humanities?

The last book I wrote before this one was called *Searching for the Anthropocene: A Journey into the Environmental Humanities*. The book is a *search* of sorts, and I suppose it's a *journey*, too. But my editor actually came up with the subtitle—and truth be told, to me it felt like a red herring. I'm not complaining about my editor, whom I trust entirely: he recognized that the term "environmental humanities" was an effective way to market the book to a burgeoning academic audience. The book might be a performance of the environmental humanities, if that means that it shows me (the author) pulling together various texts, concepts, and quotations largely from the humanities in order to make an environmentally attuned case for what it feels like to live in the Anthropocene.

But does my book define or explain what the environmental humanities *are*? No, not really. The journey is personal, associative, affective, and even whimsical at times. Maybe the book is a *demonstration* of an environmental humanities approach—but it does not delineate what this thing *is*.

So what is this, the environmental humanities? It strikes me that when we use this term, we always implicitly mean the environmental *disaster* humanities. Environmental humanities stands for the recognition that there's a problem (or many intertwined problems) with respect to the environment. When scholars work under the mantle of environmental humanities, they are generally at least tacitly operating with an awareness—and often a sense of urgency—about the ecological catastrophe taking place around us. There are animals and insects and trees and land and water that require attention, research, intervention. Species extinctions, climate change, rising sea levels, toxic excretions and spills, land use, borders, migrations, waste accumulations—all these things fall under the purview of the environmental humanities.

But what about the *humanities* part? What differentiates this work from environmental *studies*? Are the environmental humanities a mere softer subset of environmental studies? The humanities aspect of this is, from a close-up perspective, simply a way of denoting what specific academic disciplines or approaches we are talking about: history, philosophy, literary criticism, religious studies, creative writing—these might all justifiably fall under the heading environmental humanities, if the topic of this work ventures into the previously mentioned topics.

Really, it seems to me that where the environment comes into play, and what differentiates this work from other humanities work, is that it takes on an importantly *public* dimension: environmental disaster is something that no one escapes (though certain populations may feel it more quickly and intensely than others, due to class status and/or geographic location). Environmental disaster is something that the public needs to know about, very soon—which is why the academic work is done . . . and *published*, often with at least a desired level of higher visibility than might be sought after for typical academic research. It's writing and research to be shared, in such a way that might cause people to change their consumer behaviors, vote differently, reassess their relationships to the planet and other creatures, and so on. This is where I wonder if environmental humanities and *public humanities* are really two sides of the same coin. I've thought about this a lot working on the series I founded and coedit called Object Lessons, where we've published numerous short books that I've often described as being environmental humanities texts—*Earth, Waste, Whale Song, Tree, Dust, Rust, Egg*—and which are also public humanities texts. Our books are designed, marketed, and (mostly) written with a wide "crossover" audience in mind—in other words, they can be taught in first-year seminars in college and used as reference texts for certain niche fields, as well as be read and sold in museum gift shops and indie bookstores. Not all of our books in the series are environmental humanities texts, I suppose, but all of them are public humanities projects. Though pushed just a little, I'd probably concede that they all are environmental humanities, books, too. I mean: phone booths, hoods, high heels, hotels, shipping containers, cigarette lighters, traffic, golf balls, refrigerators, Walkmans, magnets, bread, jet lag . . . you can see how these ordinary objects begin to make up the extended phenotype of our species in such a way that they become, cumulatively, something like an environmental studies super-project—but carried out in disguise, sort of, as a collaborative public humanities endeavor.

But wait. Why did we need to double down on the humanities and make them public, in the first place? Weren't the humanities supposed to be, I don't know, about ordinary *humans*? Weren't intro to philosophy and history and even literature courses supposed to be about giving students a pretty basic and accessible foundation in where they came from, how they think, and how they express themselves across time and cultures? Shouldn't the humanities be de facto a turn toward the public, or better, toward *publics*?

When the Modern Language Association's *Profession* journal put out a whole issue dedicated to the public humanities in 2019, I was at first delighted—because I do think this is a really important part of scholarly work that often gets forgotten or even sneered at: making our work more accessible and less abstruse. But as I read through the issue, I became a bit dismayed. It seemed as if the net effect was turning public humanities into a reified Thing, a Thing that could be studied carefully and practiced rigorously. A Thing that could be reflected on in MLA publications. In other words, it seemed as though the result of this interest in public humanities was to have created a piece of research and writing that would not be consumed by a public audience (even if it interested such an audience, which is itself doubtful).

Funnily enough, plenty of writing is happening that is public and humanities—it's often called *literature*. Novels, sure, but also histories, biographies, and other kinds of nonfiction books. Then there are films, TV series, and other forms of popular media that do similar work. People are constantly producing and consuming and talking about humanities-type stuff that is made from the outset *for* the public and which publics reflect and reflect on. They've been producing such stuff for centuries.

And it is this kind of material, too, that environmental humanities projects often end up dealing with. Environmental humanities projects often look at how Earth's diverse ecosystems and multitudinous species are represented in or deployed or contested by various cultural texts, discursive systems, social arrangements, or events across space and time. And presenting the lessons therein, so we might learn from them and redress or even avert various kinds of disasters. Environmental humanities people are usually just really good historians, philosophers, literary critics, religious studies scholars, or writers of one sort or another who have realized that the material around us is not separate from the planet, but rather that it, well, *matters*. And they show us how.

So I end up thinking maybe the best way to continue (and continue to promote) environmental humanities work is not to create T-shirts or centers or institutes or associations or otherwise reify this thing by name (maybe not even in book subtitles!), but rather to recommit to the work we've been doing all along, studying and writing about the topics that interest us and which take us back to the disaster(s) at hand—and publishing this work so that it gets read and shared, and talked about and acted upon. I guess, to be blunt, I wouldn't want to see environmental humanities (or public humanities) become like Digital Humanities, which spiked a lot of early interest but then spiraled out into . . . I'm not exactly sure *what*, but certainly not the panacea it was supposed to be ten or so years ago. It became a scholarly meme and something of an academic parasite living off the Silicon Valley juggernaut. There is a lot of good work done under the DH banner, but the energy around it was almost impossible to sustain—and it created a lot of fumes.

Environmental humanities is environmental disaster humanities, and as such it is public humanities. But always throughout it is the humanities at its most basic and best, which is about reminding people what matters—*and* serving as a discursive zone where "what matters" can be debated and reconsidered, assessed and imagined anew. We're at a critical flexion point right now where such assessment and imagination are necessary, and so those of us who have found ourselves in the realm of environmental humanities have our work cut out for us. But from a holistic perspective, there couldn't be a better or more important place from which to teach, think, write, publish, and act.

8

Public Humanities?

Alongside the environmental humanities, over the past fifteen years or so my academic career has gradually drifted into this other field, too: what Jeffrey Williams identified in *The Chronicle of Higher Education* as one of the vibrant "new humanities" areas: the public humanities. According to Williams, the public humanities "revolves around a push to publish on otherwise specialist matters in mainstream magazines or newspapers, to engage with community organizations or other groups, large and small, and to promote the academic humanities more widely."

As I mentioned in the last chapter, my way into this came from founding and editing the series Object Lessons. The project started with the idea that scholars often know a lot about a single thing—and using that as a constraint, combined with a fixed concise word limit and an expectation for jargon-free writing, they might write books they'd really want to write if given freedom beyond certain (often arcane, even mythic) academic strictures. Our books are published and distributed internationally by Bloomsbury. We also partnered with *The Atlantic*, where our shorter essays are published. My coeditor Ian Bogost has been at Georgia Tech, and his students help on the essay side of the series. At Loyola, I teach an editing and publishing class based on the series, and I also employ student assistants to help me with the various daily tasks that the series requires.

As of this writing we have published over 60 books in the series and over 250 essays at *The Atlantic* online. The series has been an exciting project, one that we've figured out as we've gone along and which has ended up involving so many individuals and entities—a far more intricate network than I'd ever anticipated. We get anywhere between ten and thirty pitches a week for essay and book ideas, and they continue to surprise and delight us—even though we have to reject the vast majority of these pitches. It turns out that it's wildly appealing to writers of all stripes to focus on a single thing and seriously reflect on it, in writing.

I was intrigued, then, when I learned about the new National Geographic TV show *The World According to Jeff Goldblum*, which premiered on Disney+. I had to see what it was about. It's a pretty good show, wherein none other than Jeff Goldblum decides to take a deep dive into whatever phenomenon or topic has caught his attention. Early episodes were on sneakers, ice cream, denim, and so on. The show, in short, is a lot like our series—but with Jeff Goldblum narrating cleverly and donning fabulous outfits.

But as I was watching *The World According to Jeff Goldblum*, I kept getting distracted by another show being hawked relentlessly within the Disney+ ecosystem. This was *The Mandalorian*. In fact, Jeff Goldblum's hot takes began to feel a bit ramrod and formulaic, while *The Mandalorian* captivated me with its slower pace, its fidelity to early *Star Wars* details, and the way it brought back and lingered on some of the more obscure characters, like the underrated droid EV-9D9, last seen in the recesses of Jabba's palace, in the 1983 film *Return of the Jedi*, or the merciful, meditative return of an Ugnaught, those porcine scamps who got short shrift in 1980, in *The Empire Strikes Back*.

Speaking of *The Empire Strikes Back*, here's a funny coincidence: the painter of the original Boba Fett costume, Sandy Dhuyvetter, aka "Momma Fett," lives in my hometown in northern Michigan. (She plays the accordion at a local restaurant on Thursday nights.) Sandy was trained as an illustrator and visual artist before swerving into costume design in the late 1970s. Sandy's original Boba Fett armor fabrications partly inspired the Mandalorian as we know him today.

What's this all have to do with the public humanities? Well, it has to do with *design*. Not "design thinking"—just *design*. A key part of the Object Lessons series has been the design, which our editor at Bloomsbury, Haaris Naqvi, understood immediately, long before we ever launched. Haaris introduced us early on to a book cover designer in London, Alice Marwick, who took on the job and came up with concept sketches for the series design and logo. One of Alice's early mock-ups for our series design was a striking design of a wave. In this simple but elegant image, I could see the shape of the series. We haven't done a book on waves, yet, but we *do* have a new book on *Ocean*, by the inimitable Steve Mentz, who writes about the *blue humanities* in his book—an even newer humanities to come, perhaps, what with the rising seas. The cover of his book reminded me of that early concept cover.

When Alice presents us with cover concepts, it's a detailed and lively process. We see the new cover options alongside all our other covers, for the sake of comparison. For instance, for Sheila Liming's book about office spaces and office work, we had a dazzling array of *Mad Men*-esque options to choose from, in various mid-century yellows and oranges. We debate and discuss the merits of each cover option, sometimes tweaking color or placement of elements in the illustration until we have the final version. The authors also have a say in the cover design process, which I think helps us all be on the same page as the book nears publication.

So we put a lot of time and energy into design. This may sound obvious enough, but when venturing into the public humanities, design matters even more. When the objective is to communicate with general readers, framing, style, and tone can be the difference between having an audience or missing out on one. This doesn't mean that authors necessarily have to get a Design degree or learn to draw, but that they should be prepared to interact with the process—and accept design decisions made by experts, to trust the effects of good design—even when our honed critical humanities instincts might tempt us to question or outright dismiss the importance of aesthetics or surface appearance. The goal of the public humanities is to communicate with wider audiences, and so design consistency and legibility are of the essence. Not so unlike the carefully crafted *Star Wars* universe revivified in crystalline form around the Mandalorian.

And speaking of offices, and work, this brings me to another lesson. The Mandalorian is first introduced as a bounty hunter—a problematic occupation, yes, but bear with me, because the character is developed into something far more complex. To put it plainly, across the episodes he is constantly hustling, continually having to work with new people and in new settings. This is not so unlike the public humanities, which is less a unified *thing* or stable node than a cluster of various entities in motion: publishing outlets, venues, editors, authors, reviewers, social media feeds . . . in a word, it's a network requiring constant and uneven negotiations, navigations, and communications.

So not only do we publish our books through Bloomsbury and publish essays at *The Atlantic*, but we're also working nonstop on orbiting smaller but related projects: like placing an interview between one of my former students, Lauren Stroh, and the author of our book *Hood*, Alison Kinney, at Public Books, which has become a nexus for the public humanities. Or placing excerpts of our books at various other sites, like a piece from Joanna Walsh's *Hotel* at Granta, an excerpt from Susan Harlan's *Luggage* at Guernica, or the beginning of Liz Losh's *Hashtag* at Lit Hub.

At the same time, Ian and I might be working on an op-ed on public writing for Inside Higher Ed, while fourteen of our authors are writing a collaborative piece for the Essay Daily. Another week might find us hosting one of our NEH-sponsored public writing workshops which spun off of the series. Or we're corresponding with the editors at similar series like NYU Press' Avidly Reads or MIT Press' Essential Knowledge or the new Duke Practices. These series that run parallel to ours make public humanities book formats legible and appealing to ever-broadening audiences, within and beyond the academy.

And that's just a handful of connections in the dispersed constellation around Object Lessons. The world is our office. It's a constant hustle, with ongoing acts of networking not so unlike the Mandalorian's incessant journey across the elaborately populated Star Wars universe. Sometimes leads go in unexpected directions or go nowhere, or end up promising more than they deliver. Early on, we were working with Roxane Gay on a terrific book proposal on *Scandal.* This was back in 2013. But all at once two of Roxane's other book manuscripts went under contract, and . . . well, the rest is history. Can you imagine how fantastic a book by Roxane Gay on *Scandal* would have been, published in 2020?!? But that's okay, we were thrilled to see Roxane take off as she has. Maybe we'll even revisit the idea with her at some point. And it's all part of this greater network of writers, editors, publishers, and readers—the *public* humanities at work.

Next lesson: the child. I don't want to spoil anything in the show, but suffice it to say that there is a young person in *The Mandalorian*—the same species as Yoda, from the original Star Wars—who becomes rather important for the narrative arc. The lesson here for the public humanities is a simple but profound one: to do public humanities work one must be, on some level, attuned to future generations. This is also why, as I suggested in the last chapter, the *public humanities* and the *environmental humanities* are two sides of the same coin: you cannot do one without doing the other, since salvaging the planet is crucial to having a public for humans in the first place.

One episode of *The Mandalorian* takes place on a quasi-ecotopian planet called Sorgun, and it features scenes of children playing with the kid, who became popularly known across social media and on T-shirts as "baby Yoda" (before audiences knew him as *Grogu*). Now I'll admit that I'm interpreting this episode pretty recklessly, but my point is that the public humanities must be aware of, and inclined toward, generations to come—attuned to playfulness, children, and the health of environments. This also means that our *teaching* takes on new significance. We can't separate it from our scholarly work, whatever that means to each of us. Our students are, in a strong sense, an emergent *public*. This will be *their* world.

One of our first titles was Meredith Castille's *Driver's License*, a spritely book about citizenship, mobility, identity, *fake* identities, and borders. When I read the initial manuscript, I remember thinking that it would make a perfect first-year common reading book for college students. Several years after it was published, Hofstra University selected Meredith's book as their first-year common reading title, and Bloomsbury printed a special edition of the book, with a letter from Hofstra's Provost in the front matter of the book. Meredith was invited to Hofstra to give a talk and do a Q&A with the freshmen, and it became one of these cases where the long game of our work became clear to me. Like the Mandalorian's ongoing adventure, the public humanities is usually a longer process than a single revise-and-resubmit journal article finally published; and even longer than the slog of a manuscript peer review cycle that eventually (maybe!) results in a scholarly monograph . . . which then goes to hibernate in the dark stacks of the university library. I am not against these traditional forms of scholarship—they serve their purposes—but there might also be a time and place for scholars to turn decisively toward the public and even toward emergent publics to come.

Pivoting off of *Driver's License*, the final lesson has to do with vehicles. My own writings over the years have focused on the topic of commercial air travel—airports, airliners, runways, jet bridges, and so on—so I couldn't help but take a keen interest in the Mandalorian's ship, the Razor Crest (RIP). The Razor Crest is practically a side character in the show, even at one point being tragically stripped apart and scrapped by Jawas, much to the Mandalorian's dismay—and not so unlike *The Chronicle*'s description of the humanities, if you'll recall.

But when I look closely at this ship, I can't help but see something very, very familiar. It's basically an everyday airliner, a Boeing 737 or an Airbus A320. Consider those twin engines, how it lurches through the sky—how it has to cope with icy climes. Jet thrust can seem sublime, but there is no escaping the brutal realities of winter, whether in a galaxy far, far away or right here on Earth, like the arctic sublime that frames and somewhat comically undermines Mary Shelley's *Frankenstein*. Travel is ordinary, if also laced with disastrous consequences and implications.

In fact, it's the everydayness of this ship that I think inspired my coeditor Ian to create his own visual commentary on *The Mandalorian*, by placing an innocuous McDonald's sign in the background of one of the show's promotional stills. For all the Space Western hijinks and detailed Star Wars homage in *The Mandalorian*, it's also just so *ordinary*. If you pay attention to this show, it's really just about all sorts of nitty-gritty activities and objects that the newer Star Wars movies rush past way too quickly. Characters eat, they forge metal, they play with kids, they squabble, they move around from one place to another, they communicate or miscommunicate.

In fact, it seems to me that *The Mandalorian* is really eerily similar to *The World According to Jeff Goldblum*, just set in a different universe and with a different main character. There's all the same fixation on material histories, textures and dissemination, and nuanced customs.

Could it be that they're the same show, after all? Even if not, they both give clues and lessons about the public humanities. To take on a public humanities mindset is to invite a radical openness to public things, public topics. When faced with an unfamiliar activity or too-ordinary phenomenon, you can't simply say "I don't do that." You can't hide in a narrow or specialized field, even if that's what you got your degree in. You have to be profoundly open to and inquisitive about the life of humans—even where this very boundary fades away and what counts as *human* or *nonhuman* isn't clear. This may sound overwhelming, outrageously capacious, or downright depressing. What happened to tradition, fields of expertise, the old disciplinary safety nets? They all drop away or at least fade into the background. The world is our field—even the universe.

So to recap: the public humanities is about *design*, about working with visual storytellers who can help you display your scholarship so as to attract wider audiences. It's about networking widely, making connections far beyond where you imagined your expertise led you. It's about *the kids*, the next generation—even when they're really already adults. We have to do our work for *them*. It's about *the profuse everyday*, the ordinary that expands in every direction, a humanities that exceeds our disciplinary boundaries and runs way beyond the academy. The scary thing about the public humanities is that it can feel freewheeling and radically untethered from our training, our reward systems, our expected professional trajectories.

But public humanities initiatives are increasingly being recognized by universities and other academic organizations as contiguous with, rather than opposed to, traditional scholarship. And importantly so. It's still a relatively uncharted realm, and it's rife with unexpected encounters. This is all part of the fun, the challenge, the opportunity— and part of the collaborative potential. Something to keep the depression at bay, even as it gathers like a slow-moving hurricane.

9

Skimming the Surface

In November 2019 I was invited to be the discussant on a panel at a Society for the Social Study of Science (4S) conference that was meeting in New Orleans. As I'm an English professor and can't claim expertise in either social studies *or* science, how did I end up there, way beyond my field of expertise—and why did I say yes?

Anthropologist Lisa Messeri and I had been on a panel a year earlier at an International Association for Environmental Philosophy conference at Penn State. Lisa was presenting from her recently published book *Placing Outer Space*, and we were joined on that panel by architectural historian Fred Scharmen, who was presenting work from his new book *Space Settlements*. And I was presenting work from *Searching for the Anthropocene*, looking at how a range of texts imagined life on another world. We were all disciplinarily out of place, on that panel, but it was great fun and I think we all took a lot away from it. The panel had been organized by philosopher and friend Margret Grebowicz, who always has a keen sense of how to get interestingly different thinkers together, whether in her own writing or at conferences.

Back to the conference in New Orleans. Lisa had organized a panel called *Skimming the Surface: Re-thinking "Deep" Analyses*, which was inspired by writings of Sharon Marcus, Rita Felski, and my friend and coeditor Ian, among others, to rethink science and technology studies (STS). The panelists were anthropologists of an STS ilk; I had never been to a conference like this before and wasn't sure what to expect. But the experience was delightful, and it caused me to think that more academics should become "conference nomads," as I described the feeling to Jason Weidemann of the University of Minnesota Press when I chatted briefly with him at the book exhibit. (In fact, I've felt a bit like a *disciplinary* nomad my entire career, so perhaps this is just an extension of that feeling.)

The 4S conference theme was "Innovations, Interruptions, Regenerations." In the spirit of that slogan, I turned my response to these papers into an invitation for scholars to go to a conference outside their proper discipline: to engage with thinkers who may share interests and questions but have different ways of going about them. I realize that plenty of academics do this instinctively, already; but I'm also fairly certain that even more academics have never thought to do this or haven't considered how it might be beneficial—for themselves as well as for the profession at large (and for the betterment of teaching).

This was our panel: Patricia Alvarez Astacio, in her paper "Surface Analytics: Negotiating Indigenous Textiles for Ethical Fashion Manufacture in Peru" took us behind the scenes of the alpaca wool clothing and fashion industry, revealing a fascinating arrangement of actors and objects, which resembled something like an indigenous flat ontology. Sneha Annavarapu, in "Bumpy Roads, Uneven Surfaces: Experiencing the Road in Hyderabad, India," presented a moving ethnography of auto-rickshaw drivers in Hyderabad and the potholed and sinkhole-prone surfaces that these drivers traverse each day. Jonathan Shapiro Anjaria followed with a topically overlapping paper called "The Feel of the Road: Cycling and the Futurity of Surface Readings," which focused on cyclists in Mumbai. Finally, Lisa shared new work on the shapes and surfaces of VR technoculture in her paper called "Technological Façade: Virtual Reality, Los Angeles, and the Illusion of Depth."

I read the papers for this panel over the course of a normal workweek, which involves my own bicycle commute across New

Orleans, from my home in Mid-City through four miles of patchwork neighborhoods and industrial parks, and over the I-10 to my university's campus in Uptown. The route is idiosyncratic and involves harrowing intersections, choked overpasses, and spontaneously shifting gravel fields. It's basically a cyclist's worst nightmare. But these rides provided me apropos time to think about the *surfaces* that I traverse each day and to rethink the relationships between critique, deep analysis, and skimming the surface as they played out in the papers on this panel—as well as in my daily life, my teaching, and my own recent scholarship and writing. Jonathan Shapiro Anjaria articulated such a comportment in his paper as such: "The cyclist rubs cross the surface, [their] imagination of the city and its possibilities animated by the bumps and textures of the road."

I had been thinking a lot about *superorganisms* in the months leading up to the conference. Termites especially, as they are so fecund—and generally despised—in New Orleans, but also some stones that can be found in my childhood home of northern Michigan, called Petoskeys. These are honeycomb-patterned fossils from a coral reef-type organism that existed some 350 million years ago, in areas that are now covered by Lake Michigan. They are treasured up there, and often polished and turned into jewelry or other knickknacks. People love them, unlike the termites around here, even though theoretically their collective behaviors and structural accumulations are comparable. Superorganisms are vast and intricate, millions of individual units that together comprise larger shapes that appear startlingly different from any one single organism.

From a slightly zoomed-out or tweaked perspective, *humans* become clearly visible as a superorganism. Time-lapse videos of cityscapes make this all too plain. We swarm over urban space, elaborately constructed but equally susceptible to subterranean forces and atmospheric currents. When the surfaces of our streets in New Orleans flash flood, as they increasingly do, our superorganism function becomes vivid: humans and their vehicles clambering for dry ground, not so unlike our neighboring ants that stream up and out of their no less carefully fabricated mounds when rain is imminent.

As I pedal over the highway on my rides to work, I look down and see the streams of cars and trucks inching toward downtown and speeding along in the other direction. This is a way of grazing over the *surface* of the superorganism or really multiple surfaces—the textures of the road and the vehicles interacting and enmeshed. Of course, the claim of *this* as the skin of a superorganism is anathema; the standard view would hold that this is rather the beating heart of modern progress: a decently maintained highway and all its self-important mobile subjects. But, as Lisa Messeri drew our attention to in her paper, "surfaces that claim they are not surfaces" are some of the most interesting and critical to ponder.

I recall one morning when I stepped outside my home, and I looked over at a sinkhole that had been expanding slowly by the curb. Right at that moment I saw a large rat climb up from the abyss; the rat looked around, sniffed and surveyed the scene, and then climbed back down into . . . wherever. Sneha Annavarapu's paper described how sinkholes reveal "a leaky hollowness under the surface"—and this realization was vivid to me in that moment. Surfaces are always multiple, layered. What was my home but one fragile, temporary strata among many others?

When I told my son Julien about the papers I was reading for this panel, he seized on a particular juncture: "What would happen if you were in the Virtual Reality world, and you stepped into a sinkhole?" My first reaction was that this was a supercool idea: the notion that you could explore the deep and alien interiors of a sinkhole using VR technology. But when I started to express my enthusiasm to Julien, he cut me off and corrected me: "No no no, I didn't mean that. I meant, what if you were using Virtual Reality and you *actually* stepped into a *real* sinkhole, by accident?" As Lisa Messeri reminded us in her paper, when it comes to surfaces there are usually "multiple stories being told." Whereas I was imagining an Anthropocene VR sublime, Julien was attuned, to borrow Sneha Annavarapu's words, to "a story where the unevenness and bumpiness of existing road surfaces matter." Julien has grown up around real sinkholes, has been warned not to play around them or fall into them. It's no simple matter of exploring them in VR.

Back to Lake Michigan, where the ghosts of Petoskey stones lie scattered, another superorganism gone defunct. The spring of 2019, as the ice melted and higher than normal water levels were measured, it was reported that the lake had risen 31 inches from the previous year. *31 inches, across 22,394 square miles.* Let that math sink in. Or rather, let that huge number submerge you. A sweeping 31-inch surface of expansion, mind-boggling to contemplate. Locals said it was probably cyclical or had to do with more snow than usual late in the winter. I never heard anyone mention the possibility of rising sea levels, which of course affect the Great Lakes. Climate change denial runs broad and deep, across the surface as well as far into ideologically entrenched mindsets. What dialogue there is is scant and rarely developed. Yet, Patricia Alvarez Astacio suggested in her paper that surfaces "can embody and mediate dialogue." Perhaps the bloated Lake Michigan surface is a start. If not a direct semaphore of impending catastrophe, at least the signal of things noticeably changing. (Some beach houses actually had to be moved, due to the encroaching lake levels.)

In my first-year English majors course that fall, we had been slow reading Virginia Woolf's genre-bending book *Orlando*. *Orlando* is a gender-flipping, time-traveling ruse of a text; my students seemed delighted by it, but I also noticed how they were wanting to race through it and over it—when I wanted them to go S L O W L Y. To linger on the contradictory phrases and turns within each sentence. To savor the bizarre details, the subtle hilarity. It occurred to me, reading the pieces from this 4S panel, that maybe I needed to make an appeal to my students for *surface reading* Woolf's *Orlando*. We're going slow, no doubt. But we also need to pay closer attention to the loops, fissures, and undulations in the text—or, to echo a voice from Patricia Alvarez Astacio's paper, "*It's all in the textures.*" It may seem, on first blush, like a primarily aesthetic, response-driven encounter with this literary text. But, to bring back a claim from Jonathan Shapiro Anjaria's paper, "Perhaps critique can emerge through contact with the surface as well." As Alvarez Astacio puts it, "We need to dwell on the textures—the smooth and striated spaces, the knots and tensions—and learn how to feel the affective, political, historic and sociocultural traces made material." For even a literary text is, always through and through, *material*. To learn about a superorganism is to pay attention to its contours and shapes; literary patterns are hardly sequestered or off limits.

I ended my response at the 4S panel with a few questions that I found myself puzzling over after reading these compelling papers. If we accept a certain commitment to *skimming*, what is the role or function of the critic, in relation to surface matters? When should the scholar or critic pause and *dig in*? What would comprise an ethics attuned to surface? In other words, how might we delineate a *surface ethics*? Can an ecologically attuned politics emerge from surface encounters? And would such a politics also be, by default, socially just? Finally, how might we teach our students, or urge our readers, to think and read—and *act*—with the surface in mind? Across the planet, across disciplines? This is what I took away from skimming the surface, at the 4S conference: a generative openness to new questions that come from other disciplines and which help me see my own work afresh.

10

Autotheory

One day I received an email from my PhD mentor Scott Shershow, in which he asked me if I considered my writing an example of "autotheory." I was surprised by this question in part because I had just been thinking about autotheory in the work of Maggie Nelson, and I liked this form of writing a lot—but I hadn't stopped to properly consider whether I myself was doing this thing, *autotheory*. Basically, I understand autotheory to be a style of writing that is autobiographical while simultaneously attuned to and interested in articulating the networks and connections that make the self a non-simple thing. Autotheory is a form of philosophical inquiry that keeps in mind the awkward, inescapable realities of being embodied and embedded in a wider world. When I write it like this, it sounds almost silly: doesn't *all* writing do this? Doesn't all philosophy involve this? Yes, but autotheory attempts to remain self-aware, even as it does its thing—whatever that is.

Some of my favorite texts have been examples of autotheory: Roland Barthes's *Roland Barthes*, for instance, and Kathleen Stewart's *Ordinary Affects*. More recently, Lauren Berlant and Kathleen Stewart's *The Hundreds* carries on this sporadic tradition, performing and reflecting on autotheory even if not exactly by name: in chunks or multiples of 100 words, Berlant and Stewart "tap into the genres of the middle: récit, prose poem, thought experiment, the description of a built moment as in *The Arcades*, the Perecian exercise, fictocriticism, captions, punctums, catalogs, autopoetic zips, flashed scenes, word counts" (28–9). *The Hundreds* demonstrates how "Writing throws the world together, pulling the writer in tow into contact with a slackening, a brightening, a muffling" (11). This can serve as a pithy description of how autotheory works.

I want to use this chapter as a chance to think through questions of autotheory around Maggie Nelson's writing. This inquiry turned out to open more trapdoors and passageways, spill into more woods and eddies, than I ever expected. My own writing gets implicated, *pulled in tow*, to use Berlant and Stewart's phrase. I've appreciated Nelson for some time as a philosopher working in disguise as a *writer*. Always risk-taking, never less than brutally honest, Nelson's prose writings explore some of the trickiest and most subtle parts of what it means to be human. And the writing often does this by way of noodling over some seemingly unrelated matter: an everyday texture, an ordinary encounter, or a personal dilemma or source of trauma. There's something thrilling about reading Maggie Nelson, a feeling that I've shared with many of my students and writer friends. To put it plainly: as a writer, Maggie Nelson makes me want to write. As a teacher, Maggie Nelson makes me want to teach writing. As a reader, Maggie Nelson makes me want to read. As a human, Maggie Nelson makes me want to be. It's all these things swirled together, while reading Nelson's writing.

It's difficult to compare Nelson to other contemporary writers, because there are so few who work so actively and unpredictably on the seams between genres, categories, and modes. Okay, there may in fact be quite a lot of these writers, but the results can be muddled and inconsistent. To stick with this kind of writing is its own thing. The long game is no easy practice. Sometimes while reading Nelson, I try to see the writing from a distant vantage point—say, a hundred years in the future or more—and I think that these works will be seen only then for what they really are: indicative of nothing less than a philosophical awakening. Nelson's writing puts precise pressure on all the places of contemporary human consciousness that have become numb, normalized, or accepted to be natural (or unnatural). Things that are rupturing or just on the verge. Gender, identity, belonging, care for others—all these things presumed to be at work (or even at their *peak*) in cultures that have subscribed to Progress, but in fact turn out to be painfully stultified. Nelson puts a finger on these matters and draws them in fresh directions. In other words, I think Nelson is working in ways that, while certainly acclaimed and respected in the moment, will become even more illuminated—and *illuminating*—as we continue to face the ruptures, tensions, and pressures of supermodernity, including all of the ways that the human self is being redefined, stretched, and questioned. I don't think it is too much to say it bluntly this way: Nelson's writings are unflinchingly about what it means to be a human. David Foster Wallace once said that's what good *fiction* was really about, but I think it's even more evident in the kind of *nonfiction* that Nelson writes. Some writers evade this basic question or complicate it unnecessarily, whether with aesthetics or with pseudoscience. But not Nelson.

Nelson's *The Argonauts* is a form-shattering, boundary-crossing marvel. For anyone who has wrestled with the institutionalized divides between intellect and passion, or reason and art, *The Argonauts* comes as a waft of fresh air, smashing through the seemingly sturdy walls that set apart discrete modes of thought and writing, being and being aware. And that's not even getting into the real subject matter of the book. Nelson's writing in *The Argonauts* not only weaves together some of the most sophisticated gender and queer theory; it does so while telling heart-rending stories that, finally and miraculously, come together in a way that can only be called, with utmost sincerity, *literary*. It isn't just a ruthless interrogation of identity politics but also a love story—a many-layered love story, with many twists. It is Nelson's refusal to make the book easily one way or another that causes it to be such a delight—as well as instructive. Teaching an advanced course in critical theory at Loyola, one of the final assignments for my students involved them reading *The Argonauts* as a way to untangle and chart various lines of inquiry that we had followed throughout the semester, from the nineteenth century to the present. There are not many books that can quite serve this purpose; Nelson, however, has so many pertinent questions and concepts at play throughout her book that it makes a fascinating (and utterly useful) case study for students to see theory in action—or, to put it another way, to see *praxis* at work.

Beyond the pedagogical value of this book, reading *The Argonauts* made me realize what I'd been trying to do (however more clumsily and narrowly) in my own book *The End of Airports*, in which I was trying to stitch together a cultural critique of air travel with a personal journey—all that, with aphoristic puzzles thrown in at the bottom of each page. I sent the final version of this book to my editor holding my breath, sure that he'd call me out on the bizarre artifice of the manuscript. But he took it! And it now exists out in the world, in a genre-bending realm where I like to think *The Argonauts* lingers, too: in the uncanny awareness of evolution as "*a teleology without a point*" (143). It may seem audacious to set my own book next to Nelson's award-winning masterpiece, but autotheory has to autotheorize, and this is what I feel in my non-simple, mere scriptor's heart. *The End of Airports* was something like my own paper nautilus.

Teaching Nelson's *Bluets* a few years ago—in a quite different course, on contemporary nonfiction—showed me how a book can really inspire students to want to *write*. And for would-be emerging writers, this is a real trick to figure out: not just how to write, or why to write, but how to *want* to write. *Bluets* launches from a seemingly simple constraint: a primary color. Nelson discloses a desire that motivates the book—a strange, shifting desire captivated by blueness: "Suppose I were to begin by saying that I had fallen in love with a color" (1). From this audacious starting point, described in the next sentence as a "confession," things get sublimely weird, and Nelson's curiosity with respect to the history of a hue becomes a poetic meditation on existence, eroticism, representation, and the writing process. Meanwhile, it remains a book simply about the color blue. I took great pleasure in leading class discussions about *Bluets*, because the energy exchanges between the text and the students were palpable and contagious. Next time I teach this course, I may assign each student their own color to explore and write about, drawing from the verve and dexterity of Nelson's prose. Which is to reassert: Nelson's writing has tremendous pedagogical value, even as the individual works are indisputably experimental and shape-shifting. Now that I'm recalling *Bluets*, it reminds me of Jeffrey Jerome Cohen's mesmerizing collection *Prismatic Ecology: Ecotheory beyond Green*, in which each contributor took a color and ran with it; in fact, perhaps *ecotheory* can be another word for *autotheory*.

Nelson's *Bluets* was one of the books that inspired my idea for Object Lessons. When I first read *Bluets* it jolted me with the possibilities of what such constraints can result in: a limited number of words and a specific, simple object to spring from (and return to). Of course, to achieve this requires a poet's sense of structure and concision or an efficient prose writer's gift for getting to the point. These books are not for everybody (authors *or* readers), but it has been gratifying to see authors discover our series as a possible outlet for an otherwise impossible-to-publish book; and readers who intuitively grasp the value of a small well-designed book they can read on the plane and give away to a friend or colleague. Looking back, *Bluets* influenced my vision for the series more than I probably was conscious of at the time.

The Red Parts is another thing altogether. I first discovered this book in the "Sociology" section of my campus library. And because it deals with a murder case and the intricacies of a drawn-out trial, I suppose the book's categorization makes some sense, on the face of it. But it is no less a feat of nuanced philosophical examination and linguistic boundary work—as well as deep introspection. It is a gripping story that is at turns forensic and ruminative. If it is sociological, it is so in an incredibly expansive sense, feeling the textures and probing the recesses of society that pass so often as ordinary life, yet which simultaneously hold deep secrets and unspeakable reservoirs of repression. If this book meditates most overtly on violent murder and imbalances of sexual power, it also lingers with care on love, desire, family, and belonging. If the book tells the story of a horrific crime, it also is an epic poem that puzzles over human existence at large. If Friedrich Nietzsche had been reincarnated in the late twentieth century, as a quite different person, I wonder if this is what one of his books might read like. *The Red Parts* has all the honesty, boldness, and iconoclasm of the best of Nietzsche—while benefiting from all the lessons of modernity and critical theory, post-Nietzsche.

In 2017 I wrote a book called *The Work of Literature in an Age of Post-Truth*, which ended up being about how downtrodden I was—concerning the state of literature, teaching, and language's relation to truth and the world—in the aftermath of the 2016 US presidential election. Some of the book was written before the election, but these parts were woven into a post-inauguration narrative about my own professional trajectory, and the pedagogical and philosophical aporias I felt after Trump took center stage in American life. As I think back on *The Red Parts*, I realize this book gave me a pattern—but again, unconsciously so. I was sifting through personal experiences and seemingly throwaway incidents, to make sense of what increasingly appeared to be a super sad tragedy: the crumbling of humanistic inquiry, the triumph of a sneering patriarchy. Even with the caveats that humanistic inquiry was still working out its own kinks in terms of canonicity, privilege, and access . . . it was as if the project was in an increasingly dire situation with the rhetorical reversals like "fake news" and "alternative facts." My book was like a case study of a crime—one that wasn't going to be wrapped up neatly or conclusively, probably not ever. I wrote into this void knowing I wasn't going to come out unscathed, at the other side. No, there *was* no "other side." I think I was drafting behind *The Red Parts*, even though I didn't acknowledge it anywhere in that book. It was working on my brain.

White writing this chapter, I went back to my campus library to retrieve *The Red Parts*, and as I pulled it out of the stacks I found that I had dog-eared two pages, several years prior. The first one led to an airport reference:

> I drive my mother, her new boyfriend, and Emily to the airport in Detroit so that they can fly back to California together. I watch their bodies and luggage disappear into the terminal with one slice of the sliding glass doors, pull my car away from the curb, drive around a loop that dumps me back onto the freeway, then speed along mindlessly for some time until I realize that I have no idea where I am and no idea where I am going. (169)

How did I not quote this passage in my book *Airportness*? It sums up perfectly what I was trying to get at in those pages, how airports and air travel exceed the specific spaces of flight and evoke a vast sense of modern disorientation. The second page I dog-eared had an even more eerie sentence on it: "Michigan feels, as it always felt to me, claustrophobic and haunted" (181). I had forgotten this was a book, in part, about Michigan! That's where I'm from, and I had been working on a book about Michigan for some time; and it felt this way to me, too. I was writing about being haunted by this state, where I was born.

The Argonauts, *Bluets*, and *The Red Parts*: these three books encapsulate the talent and wonder of Maggie Nelson, in prose. Another thing I have respected and been impressed by for many years is how Nelson's work has been published by a range of presses, each one suited to the topic/form/style. This pattern of publishing acuity

was most likely accidental or just circumstantial, but in retrospect it's
interesting to me. Just take those three books, published by Graywolf,
Wave Books, and Free Press—three quite different publishers with
different target markets, different scopes. Nelson exemplifies how
a writer can publish different kinds of books, all equally lucid and
poetic, with varying publishing platforms and strategies. It's for this
reason that I've recommended Nelson's nonfiction books to several
authors writing for Object Lessons, because they are examples of
different forms for different venues and audiences, always carefully
modulated with these things in mind. Maybe I'm merely projecting
or totally imagining this—whatever, call it a symptom of autotheory
on autotheory.

At first just thinking about these books abstractly, I went back to
the actual texts to consult them, to range back over their pages and
lines and words. But a profoundly disturbing thing happened, as I
leafed through them: other than those two surprises in *The Red Parts*,
I couldn't really get into these books in the same way as I had before.
They all felt dated, the experimentation within even seemed quaint. I
flipped through the pages, looking for the sparks, the "nuggets" that I
guide my students to look for and savor. I couldn't find them. Like old
embers on burnt ground, where a fire had been. What had happened
to my radical, mind-bending, inspiring Maggie Nelson?!?

Wondering what was going on here, I then went online to Amazon
to see if Nelson had any new books out. I thought, what with her
current MacArthur fellowship, she *must* have a new book out, right?
And yes, there were two! But on closer inspection, they weren't *new*
at all but old collections of poems re-released on the heels of *The
Argonaut*'s success and Nelson's subsequent genius grant. The two
"new" books were *Something Bright, Then Holes* (Soft Skull, 2007 and
2018) and *Shiner* (Zed, 2001 and 2018). Still, I ordered them both
and waited in rapt anticipation for the obligatory two days before an
ominous slate-blue Mercedes van parked hard in front of my house

and a spritely delivery agent slid a thin envelope through my mail slot. Very thin.

I tore open the brown sleeve, and the two books fell into my hand—and they were beautiful. Elegant, simple covers adorned with fractal illustrations that seemed somehow reminiscent of Nelson's thinking. I was shocked and delighted to find that the cover of *Shiner* was even designed by Alice Marwick, who designs the covers of the Object Lessons books! Turning the pages between my fingers, I prepared to be washed over with Nelson's genius and poetic verve. Instead, I found lots of poems, littered across the page and dated way, way back . . . these were Nelson's lean years, stories of breakups, hurt mentors, and injuries sustained by the author herself. I determined to read these collections, to let the work of literature do what it does best: to unsettle, or if not quite that, to simply take up space and time in the mind.

As I made my way through these two collections of poems, sporadically and without method or motive, I realized that it wasn't that those earlier prose books had become dated—it was *me*. It was my own life that had fallen out of sync with the ruptures and flashes of Nelson's writing. I had needed something in those books at those times, and I had found it there. It was okay that I couldn't get the verve back, when rereading *The Argonauts*, *Bluets*, or *The Red Parts*. Hell, wasn't this experience true to my reassessment of my own books, when I dare to crack open the covers? I wince and roll my eyes as I reread my own writing. I kind of hate it. Sometimes I find a good sentence, *maybe* a decent paragraph. But usually it's a tsunami of regrets and abject feelings: *I could have written that better! Why didn't I tighten that sentence!? Did I really repeat that word again? I should have cited that thing I left out!* And so on.

I wonder what it was like for Nelson to revisit these poems, as they were moved into reprinting? Did she bother revisiting them at all? Or did she just let the publishers do their thing? I can't imagine going through the process of having to reread my work to approve or otherwise sign off on the reprint of a book. (Not that I'd complain, of course!)

At the time that I was reading *Shiner* and *Something Bright, Then Holes*, I was trying to write my own new book, a book that I was really struggling with, struggling to . . . make *different* from my other books. Or just to make *different* in general. To push into new territory, but then—that's a terrible, colonial, dominating metaphor—the book, after all, is about the Anthropocene and so *territory* is one of those insidious concepts that is by turn the cause and the effect of the epoch that humans are responsible for. In this book I was trying to write very personally about the Anthropocene, but also in a somewhat objective way—and these approaches were staggered across two quite different topics: a *place*, my home region of northern Michigan, and the peculiar realm of air travel (and modes and fantasies of transit more broadly), which have gone by the idea of *non-place*. My editor had suggested I write this book in two long parts, and this strategy ended up accommodating the two asymmetrical topics nicely. But the overarching subject of the Anthropocene can feel incredibly unwieldy and downright intimidating, nearly impossible to say anything sure or confident about—when human confidence and self-certainty are themselves driving problems inextricable from the Anthropocene.

But as I read Nelson's poems, an interesting thing happened: little Anthropocene insights popped out. The poet describes being "Not quite at home in the world / and turning toward the terminus" ("Harbor," S, 45)—the exact (if also vague) sensation I had been grappling with as I worked on this book, a feeling of being unhoused and on the verge of seeing something bigger than me, and catastrophically so. Another poem observes how, "what you never went back for / has been loaded into a dumpster" ("Harbor," S, 46). This is an uncanny description of the work of autobiographical writing, or really *autotheoretical* writing, wherein memories are handled awkwardly as newly fabricated things, and whatever was really there is always already long gone, in a dumpster somewhere and only later (now) to pollute present space but as micro-plastics do, often invisible. It is a circuitous journey and there is no guide.

The old Romantic Sublime, even contemporarily subdued, is likewise evacuated of its power while still rendered in words:

Last night the world
turned itself
inside-out

with rain, and I hoped
the water today
would be clear

and full. But I
should have
remembered, the rain

always brings in
the sewage. Still

("The Canal Diaries," *SBTH*, 31)

The poet's hopes for a cleansing purge brought about by rainclouds are disrupted by the sewage, jarringly left floating with that enjambed "Still"—a temporal drawing-out that makes the disgusting water all the more visceral. Anthropocene water. In another invocation of precipitation, we get "On this day of shattering rain, / the planes fly low" ("After Talking Late with Friends and a Line by T'ao Chien," *S*, 56). I know this sound: the amplified rumble of jet engines when the cloud cover is low and the sound seems to ricochet off every raindrop, as if to remind us that all rain is now acid rain. To paraphrase another poet: The airplanes are flying. The Anthropocene must be happening. And if this line weren't enough to titillate my fixation with air travel,

Nelson does it again, explaining how: "Everything aims to make this journey go fast / the jet stream, the in-flight entertainment, etc" ("After the Holidays," *S*, 43). The genius of connecting the prevailing winds to the instruments of pleasure and terror, and the miniature devices therein: how humans pass the time, *kill time*, as they ride along belching atmospher-killing exhaust into the ether.

These poetic fragments bespeak the Anthropocene, even as they also record Nelson's own life—writing, relating, connecting, misconnecting, seeking, finding, getting lost. At one point the poet wonders, after seeing a TV show about deep space, "how do we stay interested over that kind of time?" ("Second Avenue, Winter," *S*, 17). What a perfect question for the Anthropocene, where our provocations, recognitions, and wagers must take into account temporalities that defy mortal existence and self-centered gratification. But then, as if to answer this question (elsewhere), Nelson leaves us with a recipe for politics and aesthetics in the Anthropocene:

> You don't really
>
> have to believe in
> yourself, only
> in your circulation.

("Losing Heart," S, 70)

Nelson's poems infected my Anthropocene book, gave me new material for thinking through this always-thornier-than-you-think topic. When I decided to use a fragment of one of these poems as an epigraph for my book, I emailed Nelson to ask permission—thinking I might not hear back, or not in time, or be redirected to an agent or publisher. Instead, I received a kind reply a few hours later: Nelson said she liked those lines used in the context of the Anthropocene and that she "was searching for the Anthropocene too." It was an act of connection and kindness, and endeared me to Nelson yet again.

And so I am back to my initial autotheoretical gambit, a simple but true proclamation: as a writer, Maggie Nelson makes me want to write. As a teacher, Maggie Nelson makes me want to teach writing. As a reader, Maggie Nelson makes me want to read. As a human, Maggie Nelson makes me want to be, in the closing words of *The Argonauts*, "here, who knows for how long, ablaze with our care, its ongoing song" (143). Autotheory gathers all these things, in ever-turning, participatory circulation.

11

Beginnings

My colleague Kate Adams first put her finger on it this way: "I think our students are better writers than readers." I understood what she meant. Students lately seem comfortable with expressing themselves, writing down their impressions, feelings, experiences—and they are nimble when it comes to shifting expressive modes, from writing papers to posting on social media to creating video content to putting together unexpected fashion collages.

But reading is something else. The kind of slow time required for reading is a rapidly vanishing thing. Computers, tablets, and smartphones have ruthlessly colonized this time. Even *if* one finds time to sit with an open book or a journal article or essay . . . the slightest notification or stray impulse to check one's social media feed can derail reading. I feel this acutely in my own reading life—how this time has been whittled away. And my sense is that students have an even more intensified experience of how hard it is to just read.

I don't want to wax nostalgic about this matter. I remember when I was in college, in the mid- to late 1990s, how reading was hard *then*. There's more than just technology pulling attention away from the page. Mere sociality was addictively social long before social media made it seem ingrained. I recall afternoons in the library, my roommate Tyler and I essentially trying to hold each other to the task of reading—just getting the reading done—when we both were pulled in any number of directions: toward a movie we'd rather watch, a bike trail we'd rather be riding, friends we'd rather be hanging out with, romantic possibilities that beckoned. . . . But we'd buckle down and try to get through a few chapters of *To the Lighthouse*, or into Wittgenstein's *Tractatus*. We probably skimmed a lot and bullshitted our way through a fair number of discussions. But we read a lot, too, during those four years. And we *didn't* have Twitter or Instagram or TikTok luring us away every minute or more.

I could immediately see Kate's point, then, when she put it that way. Writing is one challenge for our students but reading is quite another. And when I offered to teach our modified survey-type course called Reading Historically II, I knew I'd have to grapple with this contemporary reality. We designed this sequence of courses over 2011 and 2012, to replace the British and American literature surveys that had become a standard in English departments. The idea was to make two courses—one up to 1700, another up to the present—that would be "anchored" in selected primary works (including epics, long poem cycles, novels, maybe some novellas). The goal wasn't coverage of *everything* across periods or geographic regions, but rather pinpoint deep dives into specific texts that exemplified certain shifts, ruptures, experimental breakthroughs, and so on. We weren't trying to give our students (as if) comprehensive knowledge, but rather ways to see and recognize when and how forms and styles develop and solidify.

When I set about designing the latest iteration of this course, I had the idea that I could use small chunks of text to get students to focus on the forms and textures of writing across these very different moments and areas of expression. I had been doing this in some of my other courses—for instance, in my Literature and Environment classes, I give students snapshots of environmental writing in order to see particular aesthetic or stylistic maneuvers. But for Reading Historically II, I decided on a different tactic: I would just use the *beginnings* of longer texts.

I ranged over and gradually gathered the opening pages (sometimes including the copyright page) of about thirty novels, starting with *Robinson Crusoe* and *Pamela*, and ending with Yiyun Li's *Where*

Reasons End and my colleague Lindsay Sproul's just published *We Were Promised Spotlights*. The idea was to track the development of the novel across three centuries and to see what the beginnings of these novels could teach us about this genre.

When I mentioned my idea to my colleague John Biguenet, he became very excited and said it reminded him of Edward Said's book *Beginnings*. Of course! This would be the perfect accompaniment to our class' primary texts. So for the single required text for the class, I assigned *Beginnings: Intention and Method*. This was probably a foolhardy move, in retrospect. While I loved lingering with Said's self-reflexive ruminations on novels *and* criticism (it's really an early example of autotheory), my students found the prose dense and even at times pretentious. The truth was, I probably could have just given my students a few paragraphs to reflect on, related to beginnings—instead of assigning the whole book. But I think I liked the notion that they'd be reading *one* full text, while they made their way through all the shorter beginning fragments. (Admittedly, this conceit may have sabotaged my perceived commitment to the actual beginnings, in the first place!)

Each day we would focus on the opening pages—or sometimes we'd tarry with a single paragraph—and once a week we'd discuss a chapter of Said's *Beginnings*. On a lark, and finding myself so enjoying Said's dense critical prose, I suggested that my students read the entire *Beginnings* as if it were a *novel*. So we alternated between *Beginnings* and beginnings of novels, reading across three centuries of novels until midway into the semester when everything ruptured and we had to begin again, and again, learning how to shift our discussions from the classroom to the internet. Covid-19 was also a new beginning, as several students aptly noted as our class ended.

12

Chance Meeting

When I moved to New Orleans in 2009, I heard that she lived in town. But I didn't really believe it until I saw her at my neighborhood grocery store one afternoon, carefully feeling avocados. It's Ani DiFranco! I gawked for a second and then went about my shopping for dinner supplies.

A year or so later I would end up at a friend's house for a weekend potluck, all of our kids playing together, and there she was again—this time on the couch sipping a glass of wine, her daughter leading the pack of kids. On this occasion I couldn't help myself and started blubbering about how I had analyzed one of her songs in my book about airports. (What a dork!) She looked at me quizzically and said, "What song? Did I write an airport song?" I blurted out, "Yeah, 'Arrivals Gate,' remember?!?" And she got a faraway look in her eyes, and said, "*Oh yeah . . . that song.*" Ani might have been a little weirded out by me, at that point. Many years later, when we were on more friendly terms, I was able to also tell her the story about how, when I was teaching my airports class, I accidentally played Brian Eno's "Music for Airports" on top of "Arrivals Gate"—and the result was deliciously surreal.

Our kids ended up attending the same elementary school for a time, and one day I was walking from my campus to the kids' school lugging an enormous *Norton Anthology of Theory and Criticism*. Ani was already waiting at the school gate and remarked on my load: "Whoa prof, that's quite a book." I said, "Yeah, I feel so bad assigning this book, it's such an unwieldy *brick*!" Ani asked, "How is it teaching college these days?" I didn't know how to answer such a big yet direct question and started with, "Oh, I love my students, they're so great . . ." and Ani cut right in to say, "Well you must be a great teacher, if you love your students." I was dumbstruck: it was probably the highest compliment, derived from the most basic observation. But somehow this statement was so perceptive on an intuitive level, and it buoyed me right then—at a time when I needed it. It was another chance meeting with Ani, perfectly timed.

The truth is, I had been teaching a particularly difficult theory class that semester—not the *most* difficult (that would come a couple years later) but the second most—and I was losing confidence in my professorial presence in the classroom. To hear none other than Ani DiFranco approve of my pedagogy of the depressed—this was an unexpected lifeline. Maybe not so unlike all the lyrics that had inspired me many, many years earlier, listening to well-worn cassette tapes of Ani in college.

I saw Ani at our mutual friend's home shortly after her book *No Walls and the Recurring Dream* was published, and I congratulated her on it. I was eager to read it. She let out a big exhale and said, "Yeah, man, it was like having a desk job for two years! I'd just wake up, sit down, and write. Over and over." I loved this distillation of the act of writing. No mystique, no romance. Just the brute work of it—which, at least in my experience, is so much more accurate to how it feels to just get the writing done. There's nothing glamorous about it; it's just work.

And this assessment of how writing feels synced up with Ani's refusal, throughout the book, of being labeled an "entrepreneur." Even as she cobbles together a business and an artistic practice that defies the odds, as she finds a following while maintaining her creative integrity, Ani resists the notion that what she has done is a formula for success or a strategy for self-promotion or marketing. It's something that rings true to me as I attempt to write books and edit books and teach my students how to earn a living in a creative way, without forfeiting a critical edge. Throughout her life, too, Ani DiFranco's art has been fueled by a spirit of activism and critique.

And talk about autotheory! *No Walls and the Recurring Dream* is like listening to Ani tell stories, but always with a relentless sense of self-awareness and critique. It was a joy to read about Ani's own brushes with literature and critical theory, in New York in the 1980s:

> Classes at the New School were small and took place in circles around tables instead of audience-and-performer style. They were meant to be discussions, not lectures. [. . .] My mind busted wide open with those writers' wisdom and an explosion of awareness came flooding in. Every single thing I read [. . .] was met with a resounding *yes* in my body and as soon as their words entered my mind it was as though I'd always known them. (97)

Of course, this was music to my ears. It reminded me so much of my first truly awakening class experiences as an undergraduate, even if the places and contexts were different, and mine happened about ten years later. But this revolutionary potential, this chance meeting of *reading* and *discussing*, is what still motivates my teaching today, another twenty years on.

13

Theory Today

The ad for my position at Loyola was listed in the MLA job list as "Contemporary Literature and Critical Theory." My doctoral exam period had been twentieth-century American literature, and my "designated emphasis" at the University of California at Davis was in critical theory. It seemed as though the position was made for me. I'm sure it felt that way to the hundreds of other lit and theory PhDs who applied. Against all odds, I got the job.

Loyola's English program, like many undergraduate English departments, had a "theory requirement." Even my own undergraduate institution, the Great Books-based Hillsdale College, a campus-sized rebuke of cultural relativism and postmodernism, offered a critical theory course for the English majors. I distinctly recall seniors shaking their heads as they left class, dragging their heavy Norton theory anthologies behind them. I avoided that class. Looking back, the fact that critical theory had made its way into the conservative bastion of Hillsdale was striking. It was indicative of how such a hybrid subfield—part philosophy, part psychology, part history, part literary studies, and more—had woven its way into the grain of higher education in the United States by the late twentieth century.

When I started my job at Loyola in 2009, the theory requirement meant that majors had to choose between one of several courses. There was a course called "Critical Theory to 1900"; there was a twentieth-century course featuring the usual suspects (structuralism to post-structuralism, basically); there was even a course in semiotics.

From the outside, it was an impressive roster for a relatively small department. I was eager to offer any and all of these courses.

But by the end of my first-year teaching at Loyola, I had made a motion to my department to get rid of the theory requirement for our majors. We scrapped the semiotics course from our course listing. I still teach a course called "Interpretive Approaches," which gives students exposure to theory from Marx and Freud up through postcolonialism and queer theory. I love teaching that class, and my students seem to enjoy the challenge of ranging across such an eclectic array of thinkers—digging into the prose around buzzwords they've run across in previous courses and readings. So why then did I get rid of the theory requirement in my department?

In short, I felt that theory had become something akin to an elite club—which went entirely against the critical impulse of what was best about theory. Not only that, the elite club had splintered and had become multiple factions constantly trying to one-up the others in terms of who had *the* master concept, *the* code to ideology, *the* key to subjectivity. In seminars and at conferences, I saw peers and mentors alike bullied or sneered at for uttering an out-of-fashion phrase or citing an obsolete thinker. With a few exceptions, professional associations and journals balkanized and refused to converse with one another. Theory had started to reproduce the very patterns and habits that it was supposed to help us think about and change.

I want to be careful here to not sound anti-intellectual or hostile to the kind of scholarship, writing, and teaching that—when done with care and sincere interest in the world—goes by the name critical theory. My own experiences with critical theory started in two energizing college seminars: one on twentieth-century continental philosophy and another on Nietzsche and Kierkegaard. In those courses, I didn't even know I was studying "theory" as such.

As I made my way through two graduate programs, my interest in critical theory both broadened and was focused, and most of my encounters with this heterogeneous area of inquiry were positive and generative. I funneled epiphanies and obscure findings into my own writing, and I used snippets of theory in the undergraduate classes I taught. I could tell that some of my peers were not enamored with reading or writing about theory, often because they detected the rhetorical power plays at work. And I recognized that some of the more adamant professors of theory could seem a bit full of themselves, inspirited by specters of Marx or . . . whatever. But by and large, my graduate seminars in theory were scintillating and creatively inspiring, cumulatively giving me the confidence to write a dissertation and teach imaginative courses. And the mentors who taught those graduate seminars were generous, supportive, and grounded.

While I did witness some manipulative dynamics and even the exploitation of labor in graduate school, on the whole I found *theory* to be something we rallied around and put to use—making anew and "making it real" (as my undergraduate philosophy professor Dr. Stephens at Hillsdale always demanded). That said, I also heard horror stories from friends in other departments or at other universities and was privy to dramas and in-fighting that made me realize that theory was far from an innocent, much less heroic, intellectual pursuit.

By the time I finished my PhD, I had cultivated a wary and somewhat ambivalent attitude toward theory. I was beyond excited to have landed a job where I could teach theory, but equally alert to the ways that it could go wrong. Likewise, while I still cite thinkers and theoretical ideas in my writing, I've tried to keep a sharp eye on when theory becomes Theory: a wall over which readers must climb and one which most people have no wish to even begin to ascend. And for good reason: what often seems to academics to be the most incisive and nuanced explanation of something all too often ends up sounding like gobbledygook to the general reader. Neologisms can be useful, and even playful and mind-expanding. But jargon-filled prose—the writing of it, the adoration of it—does a disservice to everyone involved. (Ugh, here comes the Sokal affair back to rear its ugly head.)

I didn't want to be in a department that contributed to or perpetuated an atmosphere of intellectual obfuscation or antagonism, not to mention haughtiness. If my students wanted to spend seventy-five minutes discussing Kristeva or Derrida, great—I was all on board. As long as it wasn't for *the Theory requirement.* As long as this sort of class wasn't perceived as the zenith of humanistic inquiry or the class that everyone *needs* to get into grad school. Down that path lies . . . something not good. Something myopic and something that can become toxic when taken too self-seriously.

I have continued to teach my Interpretive Approaches class every two years or so, but I find myself questioning the umbrella categorization of this class as Theory. I was especially alarmed when my friend Ian shared a job ad stating, among other impenetrably linked qualifications, that applicants should be "fluent in critical theory." What could this possibly mean? Is "theory" such a language that one can master and deploy as if a . . . *native?* In this requirement lurked the feeling of an elite club again, or really myriad sects vying for priority and attention. For we know that to be "fluent in critical theory" is really code for being fluent in *a* theory: a *particular* set of words, forebears, and philosophical targets.

What is critical theory today, and how should I teach it? Should I teach it, at all?

Of course I'll teach theory—as long as my students want me to, and as long as a majority of my colleagues think it's worthwhile for our students. But as long as I teach theory, I want to teach it with a healthy dose of self-awareness—as opposed to mere self-seriousness—about what sort of shifty, sometimes shady, field it is. How it is not immune to conflict or scandal, and how the ideas that circulate in the texts we read are of use only insofar as they can be translated to, and get traction in, our day-to-day lives. This is no small task, but neither is it too much to ask.

But can I still bring Avital Ronell's *The Telephone Book* into my next theory class as an interesting example of formal experimentation? What about Slavoj Žižek's smart reading of "Bartleby, the Scrivener"? Can we discuss it, given Žižek's provocative defenses of the unexpected, even the atrocious? Will my students engage Žižek's ideas or just scoff at the very idea of taking him seriously? I certainly can't show Louis C.K. clips any longer to illuminate certain theoretical insights. Even Judith Butler was in the hot seat for a while (I can't remember for what).

Obviously, those are *very* different cases, thinkers, and performers. And it's not as if we've never experienced crises in theory before. Heidegger has been a tricky one for a while, but we're more used to that quandary. Teaching Freud always requires the obligatory caveats.

But now we're dealing with thinkers who are still alive—thinkers who have written good things and then sometimes said or done not so good things. And they leave us questioning. How are we to teach contemporary thought with full knowledge that a star today might be sunk tomorrow? How can we—can we?—divorce groundbreaking ideas from their ground-bound authors? Is this the same dilemma as separating the art from the artist and the risks therein? I'm not sure, but downplaying the role of "theory" (along with that of the "star") is an important first step.

The humanities are not really ablaze, as they are frequently called out to be. They smolder on, with most of us just continuing to do the work, day in and day out. Even as new academic hoaxes seek to question or discredit emerging domains of inquiry, and as field-changing thinkers shift into the evenings of their careers, most instructors are simply marking papers, preparing for discussions, and working on books and articles in progress. So today's sunset is tomorrow's sunrise, when the students will show up for class again. And I'll be there to teach them, at least for the oncoming, uncertain years.

But then, maybe those uncertain years are getting a little *too* uncertain. The last time I taught my theory class, my students were on the verge of mutiny practically from day one—and it felt as though we might not make it through the semester.

Students were triggered, upset, on edge, uncomfortable, anxious . . . and not in the ways that this may sound, in the abstract, pedagogically *useful*. We were reading a lot of the same texts that we always had read in this class—from Marx and Freud and Fanon to Foucault and Anzaldua and Berlant. But something was different, this time around.

Things were *offensive*—such as Joan Riviere's descriptions of women in case studies from the 1930s. I tried to explain that what they were cringing at in Riviere's writing—demeaning, reductive explanations of womanliness as a masquerade—was part of what would lead to later (more empowering) theories about gender, sexuality, and identity. We had to put Riviere's writing in historical context. But my students seemed not to trust me. As if I were part of a conspiracy to maintain hurtful rhetoric and pernicious systems.

That was early in the semester, and things did not get easier even as we got to more recent texts. One thing that struck me especially was how students were alarmed by the often playful, provocative prose of thinkers like Gayle Rubin and Donna Haraway.

I realized that in the contemporary moment, sardonic humor and apocalyptic rhetoric have become tools of the political right; but in the 1980s and 1990s, such language was a tactic of the progressive *left*, used to destabilize normative power structures. Part of what was getting lost in translation was that my students were living in a world where they felt constantly threatened by leaders who undermined their notions of identity and futurity, often by loud ridicule and mocking.

Well, I was living in this world, too. A world in which it seemed as though earnest conversation about positive change forward was always on the verge of getting hijacked by nostalgic sentiments that were really about keeping a few people's fortunes intact. And the easiest way to critique emergent identities or politics was to scoff at them. Critique, in other words, had become conflated with a certain *tone*, and it was this tone, I think, that my students were put off by in some of the later readings. But it was also the way I taught this material. Or didn't exactly *teach* it at all, but wanted to *entertain* it, as my mentor Scott Shershow once described it. To be unsure, uncomfortable, even entertained—to be open to all this, together.

But the world we inhabit now doesn't exactly suit itself to these squishy comportments. It was one thing to attack people on Twitter or feign smug knowingness in such an online realm, but quite another thing to reflect on our vulnerabilities and uncertainties while sitting in a circle all trying to (1) act like professional college students (and a professor), and (2) as one of my students put it, "keep our very real shit together" for fifty minutes.

How I long for a classroom environment that I'm not sure exists— or even *can* exist—anymore. Now I'm trying to turn this longing into a different kind of vision, a different kind of practice. And the Covid pandemic sped up this transition and thinking, at least in my own mind. But I'm not yet sure where it's leading. It's a case for critical theory, I suppose—a *crisis* that requires thought. Back to the classroom, on Zoom if not in person—let's get to it.

14

End Meeting for All

In high moments during the pandemic, I feel like I'm doing some of the best teaching I've ever done: I carefully select a couple poems just published that week (it's for a Gen Ed course called "Contemporary Poetry"), I log on to Zoom and my students appear there—who cares if only three out of twenty show their faces?—and we read the poems out loud and then discuss them. We listen to poetry. We talk about lines and words and phrases. We have epiphanies together. We make knowledge. After an hour or so of being there, awkwardly but earnestly, we wrap up and wave bye to one another and—END MEETING FOR ALL, a few faces frozen in the last split second.

I finish these classes feeling like I know how to distill what I do down to its essence: to inspire my students to tarry with literature and entertain one another's ideas. I feel a bit guilty, though, to be honest: I'm doing this from the comfort of my home, in a T-shirt and surf trunks, barefoot. I'll shift immediately from teaching to doing a sink full of dishes then taking my toddler daughter Vera for a walk around the neighborhood. When I get home I'll help my first grader Camille with her art class, assembling markers and paper and logging her on to Zoom. Then I'll come back to my computer and check email, respond to some more and less urgent notes, write some encouraging and supportive emails to a few students who are (understandably) flailing, then search around for ideas for my next class . . . and . . . that's when the abyss appears.

What is this thing we're doing here? To call it "college" is a cruel joke. I mean, on the one hand I have total trust in my colleagues that we're all trying our best to "meet our students where they are" (in the parlance) and help them through this time, this impossible duration. And I likewise trust my students that they aren't taking advantage of all the wiggle room right now, but are in fact trying to learn and gain skills. But this whole carrying on, *as if* we're all on track . . . it's sickening. It pulls me down.

15

Night Writing

The nights are the hardest—that gloomtime roughly between 1:30 and 4:30 a.m., when the mind snaps on and won't turn off. When I begin to second-guess everything I'm doing, especially with regard to teaching and writing. The minutes drool outward and my body itches in unreachable places. I can't get comfortable, the pillow is too hard here, too soft there. My brain pulsates and becomes a black hole of self-doubt. Nothing means anything. There's a certain yellow paring knife in the kitchen downstairs that taunts me when I'm in the state. (Ever since we got this yellow-handled paring knife, it has bothered me. We got it originally up in Michigan back in 2016, and left it there for summer use. But the set of three knives—red big blade, orange serrated, and yellow paring—was so pleasant to use that we decided to get another set to use down in New Orleans . . . I did this even though I *knew* that the yellow paring knife would again immediately worm its way into suicidal ideations. Something about the yellow, a Van Goghian rhizome across space and time, an abject penchant for bile.)

I have been reading Marina Benjamin's trenchant book *Insomnia*, but I can't read it at night because the reflections are too uncanny. Also, I don't really have a place to read books at night these days, without waking up others in my family. If I read anything, it's on my phone with the light turned down to its faintest level, which even still further destroys my ability to get back to sleep. But, sometimes I can get into a long article or essay on my phone and it does lull me back toward unconsciousness, as I finish it. Other times, if a paragraph takes long enough to read and I haven't thumbed the screen soon enough, the phone will shut off and I'll be plunged suddenly into bewildering blackness. This experience always surprises me, even though it's entirely predictable.

Curiously, while my own writing is one of the things I ruthlessly critique when I'm in this spiral, it's also one of the only things that can get me out of it—or rather, it's one of the things that can ease me back off the velvet edge of the maw and deliver me back into sleep. Here's how it works:

It helps to have a deadline, but even if I don't have a deadline, I can come up with something to write in my mind. A nagging question that I can mold into the faint shape of an ethereal essay. If I can start putting words together, I can sometimes land on an entire sentence that is passable, getting me somewhere. Then if I can attach another one to it, sometimes I can get up to a paragraph in my head, maybe even two or three short ones—and then, by this hazy time with any luck I might be fading back into the oblivion of slumber.

Ideally I'm able to recall a good chunk of those words and their order, in the morning. (This time, I captured maybe 60 percent.) It almost feels more like I'm writing a single long sentence—it's often one sustained thought or impression that I'm trying to follow to see how far it goes. Maybe this is why I was drawn to the impossibly relentless prose of Jacques Derrida when I was in college, when everyone else in my philosophy class scoffed or rolled their eyes as we discussed "Différance"—I couldn't get enough. I felt the same about Michel Foucault, a couple years later. Foucault's sentences weren't nearly as conditionally convoluted as Derrida's, but his observations and points were similarly layered and interlaced. Roland Barthes's prose was so much more lucid, but there was something similar there, too: a brain rush and then a following through of a *what if*. It's not quite the same "what if" that Claudia Rankine begins her book *Just Us* with, but there's a related critical burrowing or boring that some readers might mistake for another kind of boring: philosophy, poetry, history—*boring*.

The night hours can be boring in both senses, but they are more *crushing* than anything else. And yet writing—or thinking writing, writing in my head—can sometimes throw me a lifeline, help me slip out from under the dead weight, if only to dive back into the cushiony release of sleep at last, for those milky early morning final hours before the oncoming pressures of the day.

16

Less Grading

I was standing outside the gate waiting to pick up my kids from school and chatting six-feet away with another parent, who teaches Japanese at Tulane. We were talking about how the semester was flying by—it was almost Thanksgiving break—even though it also felt slow and sluggish in so many ways, being the pandemic semester of fall 2020.

"Well, it will all be over soon, the semester. But then . . . the GRADING! Ugh, the *grading* . . ." The grimace beneath her mask was obvious, even if I couldn't see it.

I remembered the grading slog: the body aches that come with scrawling on papers, rereading sentences, suspecting plagiarism or other shenanigans, adjusting grades as the pile subsides on one side of the desk and grows on the other. Then entering the grades in the computer, submitting them . . . then waiting for the nagging emails from outraged students, haggling with them over the C, the B+, the A–, their future, their past, their very ontological status.

But I don't do grades anymore. A few years ago I realized I was putting too much time and energy into this routine act—and that my students weren't necessarily benefiting from any of it. Instead, I started to ask my students to evaluate their own performance in my classes, reflect on what they'd learned, and supply whatever grade they felt they had earned. Now, admittedly my students are perhaps brutally honest and generally self-reflective—not because they are inherently better or anything but just because these values are somewhat built into the ambience of our small, Jesuit university. Some universities tend to operate on default modes of number-crunching, surveillance, and automatic credentialing that do not necessarily imbue students with the importance of the individual journey—even when highly productive individuals emerge at the other end. (These are all such clichés, and I'm generalizing recklessly. But remember, I'm trying to write this book more honestly and without a lot of filtering. But here I am using parentheses, at the end of a paragraph I've edited six times— I'm failing miserably, pedagogy of the depressed.)

The practice I'm advocating can be formally explained and justified pedagogically as a process of "ungrading," through which students come to experience their education not as primarily aimed toward an end-grade and top-down evaluation, and are rather empowered to set their own goals and then both work toward them more consciously and thus "own" their progress more than they otherwise would. (Jesse Stommel has written persuasively and comprehensively about ungrading, in ways that I find aligned with my own practices.) If there's a problem with "ungrading" as such, though, it's that it can almost immediately get re-systematized into a different kind of reward/punishment code and the students and teacher adjust accordingly and can fall back into familiar patterns. So I don't tend to use the label of *ungrading*, at least not with my students. I usually just tell my students I don't believe in grades—that gets their attention in a different way altogether. The truth is, I'm just figuring this out each new semester with my new groups of students. But dropping grades has been an enormous relief and has re-energized my teaching—and I can see how it startles but then relieves and excites my students, too.

Of course my *school* believes in grades, so we have to do them. But we just take a simple path to get there.

Some of my colleagues are understandably appalled by this practice. It may look from the outside like I'm shirking my duties to interact with my students' actual formal classwork. It's true that I no longer collect papers at regular intervals. I grew tired of writing meticulous notes in the margins that I increasingly feared no one read. I'm conflicted about this, because one of my treasured memories from my own college years is racing up the battered staircase to Dr. Stephens's office, where he'd leave us our graded papers—always with a page or two of typed notes stapled to the original paper. I probably still have most of those annotated papers filed away in my office somewhere—I rarely got higher than a "C" on Dr. Stephens's papers, but his comments were so encouraging and so sincere that they always made me want to do better on my next one and learn from his prodding. And here I am now, refusing to give my students the same attention and care.

No, that's not true. I *am* caring for my students, but the technology and forms of communication have changed. When I was a PhD student at UC Davis, I basically mimicked Dr. Stephens's grading style on papers, delighting my engineering students who were just trying to get their required literature classes out of the way. I received an email from one of these former students recently, from a class I taught in 2005: they thanked me for everything in that class and told me they were writing again. I Googled their name and a memory came back in bits and pieces, their keen sense of humor and excitement in the class. Would they have been disappointed with my new ungrading style? I don't think so.

Now, I tend to work more individually with my students—the students who want to work this way, the students who have something they want to get out in the world. My "feedback" to students these days takes place over email, Zoom meetings, FaceTime, or even text messages. When the pandemic set in, I freely gave out my phone number, since I wanted my students to be able to reach me whenever, however it was easiest. I realize this may sound over the top, but for me, especially given my abandonment of traditional feedback and grading, I needed them to know I was there for them, to help them through this time . . . a time that was stretching out like Silly Putty, feeling endlessly thin, but nothing was funny about it. But this *being available* to my students had started several years before—probably (now that I'm looking back at it) around the time that I stopped "grading" in a proper sense of the word.

In exchange for midterm exams and written assessments and formal final papers, I've opted for more collaborations with students (we write essays together, then get them published), more senior theses and independent study mentoring, and more advising—all the stuff that takes more time and is less predictable. For example, as I'm finishing this book I'm also working with one student, Andres Castro (he needed two stray credits to graduate), on an essay for *Avidly* about masking during the pandemic and face coverings in *The Mandalorian* (whose main character abides by a creed to not remove his helmet). By working closely on edits with me and with Sarah Mesle at *Avidly*, Andres is seeing the professional writing and revision process in action. Another student, Thyme Hawkins, is working on a screenplay that reimagines the French philosopher Descartes in a contemporary social media context amid the pandemic; Thyme is teaching *me* about the platform WriterDuet. Another student, Amelia Williams, is working on a thesis collection of poems exploring how marginalized voices become heard. Then there's my student assistant Kimberly Pollard, who helps me manage the deluge of Object Lessons queries and pitches, occasionally having to navigate delicate matters like rejections and redirections.

These projects are far flung and beyond any narrow or specific expertise in our discipline—but they're all creative endeavors I'll spend hours talking through and thinking about with my students, one-on-one. It's one thing, if annoying and exhausting, to chop through a pile of twenty-five papers and provide notes on each; it's another thing to talk with students individually and trust them to venture out and fumble toward larger projects and practical hands-on experience, helping from time to time along the way. This is how I justify it, I suppose. It's a different kind of teaching.

The truth of the matter is that for some reason grading was just becoming so much busy work. And not just the grading, but all the assigning and explaining and then the students churning out words that went into it: it was falling into the routine of a corporatized assembly line, assessing outcomes and measuring performance on a stale rubric. It wasn't the time-warping, mind-expanding experience that I wanted it to be for my students, that it *should* be. Eula Biss puts it this way in her book *Having and Being Had*: "The labor of teaching, which I love for its transformative power, is accompanied by ordinary paperwork and the work of being an employee, which is more toilsome than the work of teaching" (100). I agree, and it was these latter things—the paperwork and measurable business of entering grades into forms—that I wanted to do away with. And so, no more grading.

Lest this seem totally reckless, I give my students fair warning when we start the term: I say that I don't do grades, it's up to them to grade themselves, and that this is not for everyone. Each semester, I have one or two students who drop because they don't like the sound of it. But those seats are immediately filled by students who can roll with this. I check in with my students nearly every day and make sure they're getting what they need from the class. Though, do students really *know* what they need from a class? I sure didn't, at eighteen or twenty-one. But I knew to trust my professors. Even when I didn't like them. At least, I trusted them *most* of the time. There were some incidents of recalcitrance. It's funny to look back on my years as a student, and then my years teaching, and realize how a thread of resistance has been woven through it all. Maybe that's why I was drawn to *Pedagogy of the Oppressed* instinctively, when I first saw it on the shelves of a used bookstore in Tempe, Arizona, in 2000. Coincidentally, a few years later my great friend in graduate school would turn out to be Dan Glass, whose father was Ron Glass, an educational philosopher who worked with Paulo Freire and was in direct lineage of his revolutionary methodology. So, that makes me, what, three degrees removed? It feels like it, anyway.

Grades play into the "banking" model of education, which alienates students' ability to create, imagine, and improvise—to change the current conditions of existence. Grading dehumanizes students (and teachers), because it alienates them from knowledge and their learning—the tools that can actually help people work on the problems of everyday life.

So: no grades, except the ones that students give themselves. Feedback in customized settings, only on real things that students choose to work on. Collaborative writing, instead of faux-sole-author paper assignments. (Come to think of it, I can trace this particular thread of resistance back to my Professor Linda Karell, at Montana State University: her class on collaborative authorship blew my mind and changed how I approach writing, forever.)

But how many students am I letting slip through the cracks? Too many, I fear. By focusing on my energy on the ones who want to play in this indeterminate realm of co-creative thinking and writing, am I failing to catch others? Would it be better for me to revert and assign papers, grade and write on them again, in order to widen the net and capture the interest of students who might otherwise just slip away? And is my non-grading philosophy here more a cop-out than a revolutionary pedagogy? Am I really serving my students, by refusing to partake in the traditional back-and-forth of teacher and student, assigned and graded? Could I even *go back*, if I wanted to? And what comes next, if not? How do I cultivate my non-grading method, in a world of fewer tenure-line faculty and an eroding foundation of the intellectual project to which we're supposed to be dedicated? These questions keep me up at night, leading me eventually back to visions of a yellow paring knife. I'd better keep thinking, keep writing, keep teaching.

17

Tenure

I presented a brief statement to our faculty senate, as a response to an alarming report about my university's increasing reliance on non-tenure-track faculty. As I was finishing this book, it occurred to me that the writing was part of my project here—part of the pedagogy of the depressed, because my words were subsumed into the void of higher education turned into upper administration. Here's the statement:

When I started at Loyola in 2009 I joined a flagship English department, with nearly 200 majors and 16 tenured or tenure-track faculty. We excelled in the areas of literature and creative writing. In the years that followed, the department launched an exciting new third track to our major: a track in Film & Digital Media, capitalizing on what were then emergent trends in the Digital Humanities.

This major attracted lots of student interest, not surprisingly. However, after losing several key members of the faculty who taught courses in the track, and not being given replacement hires, the Film & Digital Media track has languished. Now, with three of my senior colleagues retiring in January and no hopes to replace these critical faculty members with tenure-track positions, this puts our major track in Film & Digital Media at risk. Losing this track would be a real loss for our students.

Our department houses the fifty-one-year old literary journal *New Orleans Review*, as well as my book series Object Lessons. Through these two entities, our undergraduate students get unparalleled experiences working on real-world editing and publishing projects.

We've seen our students go on to excellent paid internships and eventual high-level positions in the publishing world on both coasts. And so just last year, our department launched a new Center for Editing and Publishing—unique for our region—which includes a certificate in editing and publishing that we give to students who complete five hands-on, practical courses in this professional realm. In its inaugural year, we awarded eight certificates to excellent students who will most likely go on to successful careers in editing and publishing.

But here again with the loss of key faculty, and with no promise to replace them with actively publishing, research-driven new hires, this important growth opportunity in the Center (and the certificate that comes along with it) is also at risk.

And then there is what hiring means to a department: hiring isn't just about obtaining new instructors to staff existing courses. Hiring is about coming together regularly in the spirit of comradery to articulate vision and to build a department geared toward long-term commitment to our students. Imagining new courses. Increasing diversity. Showing our students that we're moving forward, not just standing still. It's also about including our students in the dynamic experience of growing a program and defining who we are— something that is now part of them, something they'll take forward through their lives, as graduates of Loyola English.

In January 2021, my department will be down from sixteen to six tenured or tenure-track faculty—far too few to adequately develop our programs and mentor our majors. When we're not hiring tenure-track faculty, we are not doing our students justice.

And what about research? We are supposed to be a *university*, after all. When we don't hire faculty whose job it is to actively research and publish, our courses and programing cease to be current, and departments cannot stay on the leading edges of disciplinary knowledge production and dissemination.

Tenure-track research is about exercising academic freedom to confidently develop programs that our students will recognize as innovative and fresh—but stable, too. When we stop hiring research faculty, we erode the very core of the university. And the effects, while perhaps only gradually evident with the time lags that will occur due to student and faculty attrition, will be catastrophic for the intellectual life of our campus.

*   *   *

No tenure-track hires were granted in our college that year, even though the university did hire several administrators of various nonacademic departments and units.

18

Exhaustion

Maybe what's so depressing about all this is that it feels very much like living at the end of something. I tried to write this section in my awake hours last night and ended up giving myself nightmares: my campus was in postapocalyptic ruins, the lettering of LOYOLA UNIVERSITY on one of the buildings was crumbling off, L O still there but then the Y tipped on its side dangling, and the rest of the letters scattered on the ground strewn with trash. A group of students brawled behind a fence, and a shaggy German Shepherd snarled through a crack in a brick wall. This scene went on for impossibly long, in my dream. I was merely walking across the quad, to get to my next class, and I was terrified not necessarily by any of these details but by their cumulative ordinariness.

I have been trying to figure out when things started feeling so bad. Of course, the corporatization of higher education has been a long creeping process, in no way a new thing. I'm only registering the latest forms and manifestations of this, from the adjunctification of faculty to the digitization of learning. The pandemic accelerated both of these, making universities like mine more financially skittish than ever, thus offering buyouts to tenured faculty with no plans to replace them, and also ushering in new hybrid modes of learning that turn out to be "flexible" in a calculated way: for saving money while maximizing potential reach.

It is predicted that in the next decade or so, somewhere between 500 and 1,000 small to mid-size colleges and universities will close— not a direct consequence of the Covid-19 pandemic but hastened by its ripple effects. Loyola is arguably in this hypothetical 1,000 range, though our relatively new and very savvy president, Tania Tetlow, assures us that we are not at risk, because of our endowment which remains around $200 million (not huge for a school of our size but still a significant amount). We are also in New Orleans, which until it floods for good will continue to attract a diverse population of students from around the country and increasingly from around the world. Finally, we've got our Jesuit identity, which besides being a fairly reliable "brand" is also a real tradition of intellectual pursuit.

That final point, the intellectual pursuit, is what makes the current condition of teaching and scholarship so depressing. It has become clear over the past few years that universities are far less interested in critical inquiry and creative thinking than they are in assuring student satisfaction, retaining students at all cost, and staying certified through byzantine assessment measures. This general shift in priorities seeps into the classroom. Students identify as customers and treat teachers as delivery agents.

I've tried to stay positive in this job. I've had fruitful collaborations with wonderful writers and teachers over the years, attended truly scintillating conferences, and participated in various strategic plans to reinvigorate our department and our university. I've kept publishing my writing and sending out new work (and getting plenty of rejections), and I continue to come up with current classes in response to student interest and excitement. I've served on so many committees for my university, reviewing award nominations and voting on tenure cases and meeting with different constituents from across campus and the community. I try to give my students real and vibrant exposure to all these things, as they develop toward their degrees.

But I'm tired. I'm tired of keeping up the charade that we're working toward real transformation, when it feels more and more like we're mostly just maintaining a cobbled together machine that's on the brink of falling to pieces. I'm tired of feigning the dumb attitude of

"What do I know? I'm just an English professor." I'm tired of making self-deprecating jokes about the worthlessness of an English degree, to my students . . . or somehow, even worse, the earnest delineating of just *how* valuable and flexible and nimble this degree truly is in the post-graduation, late-capitalist world of life and work.

I want to be able to write a constructive and persuasive book like Kathleen Fitzpatrick's brilliant *Generous Thinking: A Radical Approach to Saving the University*, a book that I find myself nodding along with as I read each sentence. But then I go to work, I see the administrators arrive in their BMWs and Teslas and park in front of the main hall, while those of us who can't afford parking passes scrounge for free parallel parking on the streets a few blocks from campus, edging our dented Subarus and Hondas into questionable curbs. I see our students tromping across the quads, stressed out and trying to take college seriously while facing uncertain economy and nebulous job prospects. I see my colleagues fading away, and the remaining few of us attempting to keep the integrity and traditions of academic scholarship and creativity alive, with dwindling resources. I want to help save the university, but I also feel like I'm getting sucked down into its bureaucratic quicksand.

19

Well-Rounded

And it's not just about me, not just about my discipline. It's not about a supposed "crisis of the humanities." This is about a widespread erosion of belief in and practice of a liberal education, where students are expected not just to grudgingly check off a list of general requirements but actually *learn*—maybe even *enjoy* learning—across a wide swath of subjects and disciplines. I am starting to realize that for years I've been operating under the assumption that we valued this mode of higher learning, a kind of education that results in "well-rounded" people. Wasn't this our shared goal, on some basic level?

The professionalization and careerification of higher education is no secret: schools worry about how they can guarantee a definitive return value to their students, when they woo and recruit them. And to a certain extent, I am interested in this, too: our English department responded to this need directly by developing our Center for Editing and Publishing, to give students hands-on experience in the real world.

But that "real world" formulation has always bothered me. It's more like I'm trying to show my students that the work we do—writing, editing, publishing, marketing—is *already* real, and they are part of it! The whole point of becoming well-rounded is precisely to be this way now and going forward. It's not an exercise or a drill: it's what we're supposed to *be*, by becoming this way. At least that's what I always thought.

We still have a "Loyola Core" which resembles what many universities and colleges require: a smattering of courses from across disciplines, from the sciences and the fine arts to the humanities and language courses. This is all fine and good, but when these courses are largely taught by contingent faculty to whom the university has shown no real, long-term commitment, then the gradual effect is one of a cheap buffet of randomized classes which stand in for a well-rounded education. This is not to disparage any of the individual subjects or instructors that contribute to this Core, but rather to question the absolute bare-minimum approach that so many institutions take to this allegedly central project of higher education. Instead of investing in faculty who will teach courses that students can build on, they scrimp for the easiest options to check off the boxes in order to pretend that they are educating well-rounded citizens.

Because that's what this is about, isn't it? It's about becoming a citizen. About learning to see things from multiple perspectives, through different disciplinary angles and using different skillsets. It's about discovering new interests, in places you didn't expect—it's about *continuing* to learn. And it's about starting this stuff *in* college, not waiting to be someone later.

This is the vexed thing about general education or liberal arts requirements in college, though: they are ostensibly central to the mission (creating life-long learners, well-rounded citizens, etc.), and yet these very classes become the bane of everyone's existence. Tenured professors tend to avoid teaching intro-level or non-major courses, if they can; and likewise, students tend to want to simply get through this stuff as fast as they can (if they can't pass out of it in the first place, with advanced placement credit or the like). So we end up with a paradox: the alleged *core* of the learning experience ends up heartless.

20

Turning Kids into Capital

One of my biggest pet peeves is hearing colleagues refer to our students as "kids." They're not: they are younger than us, sure, but they are still adults who can go to war, operate giant metal boxes on wheels, make all sorts of weighty decisions, acquire disciplinary knowledge and expertise, and work for pay. When I hear professors refer to students as "kids," I detect two things: a sort of assumed unbridgeable distance and condescension. As long as I'm a college professor, I don't ever want to be caught saying "*kids these days!*" in such a condescending tone.

Yet in his book *Kids These Days: Human Capital and the Making of Millennials*, Malcolm Harris turns this phrase on its head and recycles it into a critical phrase with descriptive power: when older generations talk disparagingly about kids these days, they should really look both inward, at themselves, and outward, at the economic substructure that made and make these kids who they are—in other words, look at the older generation and their protocols of competition and wealth accumulation.

The millennial conundrum might be explained as follows: younger people "these days" are under constant pressure to perform and to practice being on the market. Or, really, as Harris makes clear, children these days are always already on the market: working (without pay, most of the time) to hone skills, prove their worth, increase their value, and ultimately outperform others.

How does this work in practice? I remember a time back in 2008 when, in one class I taught at UC Davis (where I was a graduate student), I ditched "papers" altogether and had my students start blogs and do all their writing online: posting, linking, commenting, creating. The class was a blast, and the students impressed and amazed me with their digital prowess. And I think they learned how to write a bit, too. We'd spend our class time discussing specific blog posts they had written and talking about form, style, etiquette, audience, and so forth. And it was fun; it felt more like play than boring academic work.

But now, in retrospect, I see that this was all part of the millennial predicament, exacerbated now in the following generation. In Harris's apt description, "Play is work and work is play in the world of social media, from the workers to the users." In that "disruptive" class at UC Davis I was aiding my students' ongoing conversion into human capital.

In *Kids These Days*, Harris provides a vocabulary and a heuristic for understanding how the millennial conundrum plays out in a number of case studies and social settings, from psychotropic drugs and Big Pharma to education, youth sports, and other proto-professional regimes, to social media and the childhood celebrity complex. The research and snapshots Harris provides are engaging and astonishingly translatable.

Rather than a dry or detached study, Harris's book is a spirited romp through a disturbingly familiar landscape. Helicopter parents and "vigilante moms" are brought into vivid focus, and the timely concept of "precarity" is given flesh and bones. Harris takes readers from toddler playgrounds to tween TV shows and through college admissions, carefully charting the economic network that holds it all together. Wisely, *Kids These Days* stops short of offering any easy solution for cleaning up this mess. We end up in the thick of it, implicated and yet perhaps better able to see what's happening all around.

Reading *Kids These Days* was an uncanny experience for me. I found myself continually reflecting on my own experiences teaching at the college level—I've basically taught millennials, and now, Gen Z, since I started teaching college. From my time in the classroom and dealing with thousands of college-age students over those years, I recognize many of the troubling trends and patterns that define these generations.

I've witnessed firsthand the profusion of breakdowns, excuses, disclaimers, and stressors that fuel and beguile kids these days. Things that, when I'm speaking candidly with colleagues, we don't often know what to do with—because aren't these things merely the stuff of life, rather than elaborate medical diagnoses or personal affronts?

But no, life is more complicated these days. Capital has insinuated itself so thoroughly and effectively into the weave of ordinary life that no place is left untouched. My students have become "human capital"—and somewhere deep down, if not right on the surface, they know it. The anxieties and pressures they feel may be annoying from a professor's standpoint, but they are also completely understandable from a structural perspective. As Harris notes, "Given what we know about the recent changes in the American sociocultural environment, it would be a surprise if there weren't elevated levels of anxiety among young people" (167).

These downsides are not the only things I notice, though, when it comes to my students. I also recognize the incredible talent, responsibility, and creativity that my students exhibit—things that also feed into what Harris smartly calls "the millennial situation." It's hardly black-and-white, and it's not just about a bunch of hypersensitive spoiled brats.

I've discovered a clue about how this works at my own university. There was an increasing push to use the content management system Blackboard for more and more of the daily administration and monitoring of classes: for grading, charting attendance and participation (to better track retention), managing assignments, and so on. I was leery of Blackboard pretty much from the outset, generally disinclined to utilize its various functions for the basic reason that I'd rather not spend any more time on a computer than I have to. (As I was finishing this book my university switched to Canvas, the transition to which I discussed earlier.)

I went into college teaching because I like to sit around with a group of people and talk about things together. My students show visible signs of relief when I tell them we won't be using Blackboard (or now Canvas) in our course. (Probably because it's one less thing they have to keep track of on their phones or computers.) For me personally, if I have to be on a computer I want to be writing or maybe communicating with other authors or editors—either way, I want to be doing my *work* in a rather narrow sense: oriented around *writing*. And when I'm teaching, I want to be *teaching*.

I would prefer never to have to email students or interact with them over Blackboard but to have *all* my interactions with my students take place in person. (One can dream, right?) It's not that I'm so old-fashioned, but rather that I strongly believe that there's something immeasurably valuable—I'd almost say magical—about being together in a seminar space, in dialogue, uncertain of where our conversations are going but delighting in their twists and turns, all learning from one another.

Now that I think about it, "Blackboard" strikes me as vile euphemism for the way that it suggests being in a classroom (*real chalkboards, on a wall!*), when in fact its literal meaning involves being *out* of the classroom—and *on* a computer. And we know what "on a computer" means: that weird zone in which one stares into a depthless abyss of *work*, ever more work: surveys to fill out, company customer service emails to read or delete or just let sit there, notifications to acknowledge, commands to Buy Now, Save Big, Click Here, Act Fast, social media feeds, competing windows and tabs. . . . We know this space all too well. It's the ideal workplace for human capital because it feels vaguely personalized and (still, for now) like the *future*, like we're saving time somehow.

Yet on the computer the reality is that we are producing value with each keystroke, click, and every swipe of the thumb. Many have felt the time warp of internet browsing—that sudden awareness of "How did I end up watching YouTube videos of cats and sitting through Geico ads between clips?" In other words, what passes as "saving time" or creating more "flexible" work or learning space is really about wasting time while *producing* value—but value that goes somewhere *else*.

Just think about the very real "deliverables" that occur when students check Blackboard on their phones and when professors upload PDFs of abstruse articles. The recipients of this value are *not* those on the college campus. When scholars and students are forced to spend more time online, the inevitable beneficiaries are the tech behemoths that profit from ad sales and the aggregation of personal information. Tech companies profit while we push buttons.

In the context of rampant pushes by upper administration toward ever more online offerings, Blackboard becomes a shrewd way to shrink the continuum between in-the-flesh classes and online platforms. Ironically, such "innovative" models of higher education delivery are not being pushed for by our millennial (or Gen Z) students, but rather are advocated and championed by professionals beyond the university, as well as some of my older colleagues and upper administrators. Of course, neither do the millennial students have the agency or even the memory to say NO to the latest snake oil pedagogy.

Which brings us back to *Kids These Days*: the economic structure of the millennial generation is devised by the *owners*—that is, an older generation. This may sound obvious, but it's a key point of Harris's book. Facile complaints about how high-maintenance, hyperactive, or overworked students are: these aggravations need to be redirected to the source of their economic subjectivity, back to those who advocate Blackboard and Canvas and Google Suite and Microsoft Teams (and now Zoom) as solutions for smooth, efficient operation. So-called helicopter parents are the go-to scapegoat; but, as Harris shows in great detail, they are just one character in a much larger plot. The market is a big bully, and toys are us.

*　　*　　*

Kids These Days helped me better understand too how such dynamics exist at the other end of schooling. For example, my retired father had been substitute teaching on and off for the local school district up in Michigan. He told me about a first- and second-grade blended class in which all the children have iPads, and how as soon as the children are done with their required lessons they are allowed to use the devices to play math-oriented games. My father said he could see why iPads in the classroom are a teacher's dream: the students become absolutely quiet, plugged in, and tapping diligently at their screens for twenty minutes or so at a time. He observed this with bemusement, but I don't think my father quite grasped the insidious implications of such a scenario.

Here in the first- and second-grade classroom was the hushed, relentless training of human capital, in which students were rewarded for quick and efficient work by being slyly given *more work*—in the guise of edutainment. For we know that the true result of being on our screens is to drive the endless "growth of growth," in Harris's words, or the process of doing ever more work on behalf of the titans of Silicon Valley and the cash flows that sustain them.

At my university I teach a course called Interpreting Airports, which is an interdisciplinary seminar in cultural criticism focused on air travel. I increasingly realize that I need to take time to explain to my students why we're doing what we're doing: it's not *just* about "interpreting" airports (or anything else), but only worthwhile if we can also *change* our actions, change these places (or whatever else we're interpreting). In other words, the class isn't merely about removed contemplation. It should result in our rethinking and ultimately reshaping the patterns and trends that comprise day-to-day life. In this case, how and why we travel by air.

I'm not suggesting that college students should emerge from class with as-if quick fixes to societal problems, but rather with a revolutionary spirit instead of mere acquiescence. College students can be trained to be more intellectually reflective, and they will also jump to the task, in good millennial fashion, when prompted. But the trick, it seems to me, is how to help them dwell in the uncomfortable space between musing and action—so as then to act *differently*. In the context of my seminar this means not just griping about airports, nor merely appreciating them and carrying on, but seeing air travel gradually as something that can actually be *changed*.

As I read *Kids These Days* I felt affirmed and bolstered in my efforts. Harris sees two possible pathways for the fate of millennials: revolution or fascism. In my class when we read articles about the future of air travel—biometrics and facial recognition scans, ever-shrinking seats, travelers thoroughly reduced to "customers" (if not outright bio-cargo)—it sounds a lot like a fascist dystopia. And yet, humans might still swerve away from this model of transit toward other forms of mobility. A revolution is still possible.

After reading this book, I happened to offer a course at Loyola on children's literature and toy culture. I started the class with *Kids These Days*, so as to focus our readings and discussions on structural concerns. We read Richard Scarry's *Busy, Busy Town* and Maurice Sendak's *In the Night Kitchen* and Don Freeman's *Corduroy* and Dr. Seuss's *Oh, the Places You'll Go!* and *Harry Potter* . . . all with the production of human capital and the making of millennials in mind. As Harris makes clear through his analyses, the economic problems of this era extend to the lowest rungs of childhood management, and so it seems more important than ever to look at how the market starts to "drive us mad" at an early age, in the pages of some of the most innocuous or precious-seeming books.

We finished that course by studying the Lego Friends line. I asked each student to purchase a small set (under $10, and I helped anyone who needed it), and we built them together in class, discussing the toys as we went. It was fun, awkward, hands-on—and critical. Then we wrote a collaborative essay on these toys and their extended cultural form as a kids TV series. *3:AM Magazine* kindly published the essay, after the class was complete.

All these children's stories and playthings took on new liveliness (and some terror, too), as we thought through them with *Kids These Days* in mind.

One time in a graduate seminar at UC Davis, we were struggling with Marx's *Capital*. We were trying to understand the fetishism of commodities, or maybe how surplus value works. Whatever it was, my cohort and I were getting lost in the weeds of theoretical discourse. At a certain point our professor, Timothy Morton, said something that I'll never forget: he said, "When you're reading *Capital*, just pretend it's a mystery novel. It'll be easier to understand that way." And he was right! We all relaxed and started to read Marx for the meandering story he was telling, and the narrative build-up, rather than trying to pretend as though we fully grasped Marx's finer points at every turn.

I was reminded of this as I read *Kids These Days*, which has the refreshing virtue of being a rigorously Marxist book without sounding cloyingly *Marxian*. Harris is interested in *people*—in how actual humans are being affected by a real economic structure, right now. The story Harris is telling is as strange as Marx's *Capital*, and even stranger for taking place all around us.

Writing Together

During the pandemic summer of 2020, I was asked to participate in a teaching conference at Loyola—remote, of course, facilitated by Zoom meetings. The idea was to support our faculty as we were all "pivoting" and adopting new modes and ideas for just how to teach college in our brave new Covid world. I was slated to do a session called "Using G-Suite" for online and blended learning, but that was a misnomer. I wasn't going to be talking about the range of G-Suite applications. But I'd been using Google Docs in my classes, even before the pandemic struck and our classes went entirely online.

A few years ago I realized I didn't like developing a fully settled and scheduled syllabus and printing off a bunch of copies, only to have it all inevitably change once I met my students, expectations shifted, and hurricanes came and went. So I started creating the skeletons of my course syllabi on Google Docs, and sharing them with my students early on (in addition to posting the minimal first descriptive paragraphs on our course listing). Then I never had to print my syllabi out, much less staple them together (the cost savings alone!), and the students could keep up with the changes in real time on the Google Doc as our courses evolved. I am very clear with my students that our syllabus is a living document and that they are participants in how it unfolds—not just passive recipients or customers of a finished product.

Then I began experimenting with having my students sign up for presentation dates right on the Google Doc, so everything for the class resided at a single, fairly transparent destination. I gave all my students "edit" privileges on the Doc, so they could get on there and write directly on the shared page. Students intuitively did things like italicize their own writing or use a different font color to set apart their comments. Writing in a sort of "public" setting like this can be intimidating, at first, but mutual trust and mutually constitutive patterns of learning develop quickly. Google Docs became a way for me to imperfectly carry on the vibe of our discussion-based classes, on a blank page each day. (And these blank pages got full of sentences and ideas, and remained in one place.)

In those blissfully naive weeks before the spread of Covid became apparent in New Orleans, my class was already used to getting on the Google Doc syllabus to see what we were doing from week to week, day to day. When we all moved online in March, I told my students that we'd meet *on the Google Doc* and keep our discussions going there. I wasn't really sure how it would work, or how it would go, but I figured that since my students were already used to it, we should try the Google Doc. I did this primarily out of efficiency and simplicity: I wanted to make it as easy as possible for my students to keep up with our class without introducing new platforms or sign-in mechanisms.

My classes tend to be predominantly discussion-based and improvisational, and so my challenge was to reproduce this ambience as best I could, if in a very different format. The Google Doc is a very rough simulacrum. It is a straightforward if rather inelegant way of capturing a live discussion on the page. But it worked. This won't work for every class, obviously; it may work for certain disciplines better than others. And not every student will be able to utilize a Google Doc fully in the ways I'm describing, so the instructor always has to be prepared to offer alternative ways for students to be involved. (But this is always the case for any format, really.)

The significant change was that we were using our class Google Doc not only to see *what* we were reading and discussing but also as a forum in which to *have* the discussions: the Google Doc became a classroom, of sorts. It was also a place where we could all find the day's reading. Moving to the online realm at the onset of the pandemic, I radically stripped down our reading assignments. Or, even if I had my students reading longer texts, I would only give them a paragraph or a page to read directly and interact with on the Google Doc. I used simple screen captures a lot, to extract chunks from the texts I'd assigned—rather than handing out readings in class or emailing the students longer PDFs. I would put these screen captures or brief texts right on the Google Doc, then start off with a few prompts—and our discussion would go from there. Of course, you could also use a still from a film, a screengrab from a website, an article, an ad, a linked song or any other text to get the discussion going. The key, in my experience, is to keep whatever it is you want your students to discuss limited and concise—something they can digest within a few minutes at most.

There would often be a fairly informal conversation happening in the chat box off to the right, while the more formal discussion about the text in question would happen on the main Doc. Some students will be in a more observing mode, while others are really engaged, writing their own sentences and interacting with one another. I have them sign their comments with their initials (even though they could also be tracked through the edits history function), so we can follow the discussion from point to point. Students often get into multiple parallel conversations during one session, resulting in fruitful exchanges and respectful debates.

So, for example, in my Interpreting Airports seminar, I might start with a simple image I run across on my phone, like something at the United Airlines website: a spinning progress wheel in the middle of a clear sky, a Boeing Dreamliner cruising along while standing still, and the words *Thank you for choosing United and letting us connect you to the world*. Something mundane and seemingly straightforward.

Beneath the image, I'd seed the discussion by asking a few short questions, such as: *In what context would we find this image and text?*

What does this image/text convey? Do any details strike you as odd or curious? Explain why! Ideally the discussion would take off from these questions and their responses, and I'll be acting as the moderator, facilitator, and cowriter—accentuating students' observations and connecting their points, and demonstrating in real time how we can make knowledge and critical insights, together. So much of it is just *affirming* that they have anything to say at all.

From one perspective, it doesn't seem all that different from using a discussion board on Blackboard or Canvas. But besides being a more real-world interface than these higher-ed specific platforms, there were a lot of other practical advantages to using a Google Doc that I discovered along the way. Here are seven lessons I learned from the experiment:

(1)   Students quickly found their own ways to contribute and participate—even though these ways ranged widely from student to student, from class to class.

(2)   The Google Doc gave students lots of different ways to interact with the class: through direct writing on the Doc, through comments, through the chat area to the side of the Doc, through hyperlinks that they added, and so on. (One student added clever comments punning on various song titles, hyperlinking to the tunes on YouTube . . . so we always had an impromptu soundtrack for our classes.)

(3)   The Doc fostered active collaboration from the get-go: our classes were *always* a product of what many of us did on the Doc, together. It wasn't always the same group and usually not all of us on the same day—but that's okay. The unevenness is something to be embraced.

(4)   The Google Doc allowed for synchronous as well as asynchronous participation. For students who were able to "show up" for class, or who craved a more set structure, they

could "be there" while we asked and answered questions during the allotted fifty minutes of our class. For those who couldn't make it during that time, for whatever reason, they could get on the Google Doc later and follow the discussion that took place—as well as add their own comments, observations, or analyses.

(5) The Doc became a living transcript of the class—and a document that, by the end of the semester, the students could scroll back through and be impressed with. In one of my classes, we amassed nearly 50,000 words of critical engagement and analytic prose between mid-March and May! I told my students this was the length of a book (a *Gatsby*!), and they were proud.

(6) Following from the last point, portions of a Google Doc might be strong enough that they can be revised and polished—even to the point of being submitted for publication. I've started two collaborative projects with students on Google Docs that resulted in publication. If a discussion thread or exchange seems particularly rich, you might think about developing it with your students for a short essay; there are plenty of academic and para-academic venues that are open to publishing student-faculty collaborative work, even if it's in pithy or rougher form than proper scholarship.

(7) The Google Doc allows for a good amount of flexibility in terms of how and when students engage, and collects all these records of engagement in a single destination. It's relatively easy to search through the archive of edits or even the content of the Doc (especially by searching for initials, if you have students just initial their contributions for the sake of following the day-to-day discussions).

A big caveat, if you choose to try this: *the beginning of this process is almost always nightmarish and unwieldy*. The first few days on the

Google Doc will be overwhelming as you and your students learn to write together, write over one another, become self-conscious of invisible eyes watching and other writers ready to pounce—these things make the collaborative writing experience harrowing, and it can be tempting to give up. It will feel messy and awkward and clunky—not necessarily *productive* in any clear sense.

But if you can push through the first week or two, you'll discover that your students will gain traction, get in their grooves, and find their rhythms with one another. And you'll find that your role will become clearer as you stick with it. Also, your role will be different from course to course—not always the same, even if it's the same class and same material. You'll have to figure out your questioning-writing-editing-nudging personae with different groups of students. It's a leap of faith, but one worth taking.

At the end of my most recent semester using Google Docs, I was heartened to receive reflections from many students—even some of the most quiet students, in person—who said they appreciated the relative mellow nature of our class and being "given time to think" on the Google Doc. This surprised me because the Google Doc can feel very cacophonous when everyone is writing at the same time, a scramble of multicolored cursors jumping around the page. But maybe that's just from my slightly more removed perspective, trying to keep it all flowing and moving in a steady direction. For the students, maybe—hopefully—it really does just more quietly (if crudely) replicate the classroom with all the thoughts and observations and reactions that normally unfold, there. A space for reflecting on and saving.

22

Adjusting

Despite the drudgery of committee meetings and seeing higher education shift into something else entirely, one of the reasons I've loved my job for the past twenty years is that I cherish the ineffable experience of being in the classroom with students while learning is happening in real time. There's nothing quite like asking a student to read a poem aloud, letting the words reverberate in the classroom for a few awkward moments . . . and then asking another student to read the same poem aloud, again. More awkward silence; we look around the room. Then . . . wait for it . . . discussion erupts.

Ever since my first semester in college, there's something about this experience that has fascinated and inspired me. I live for the epiphany moments when students make a sudden breakthrough or when they connect things from different classes, across disciplines, making connections we never anticipated. There was always a palpable buzz about the classroom: the suspense of the first day of class; the midterm weeks when things are congealing and we've achieved a unique discussion dynamic; and the always bittersweet end of the semester, when it's time for final presentations and students gush with admiration and pride at their cohort's achievements, and a little sadness for the fact that it's almost over.

But I don't think it's going to be the same, from now on.

Even just a month into the online "delivery" of my classes, in spring 2020, I worried that there was no going back. It's a new kind of exhaustion and tedium, connecting online with my students. But I'm afraid that to some of my colleagues and many superiors in higher administration, it will look more like a new kind of efficiency. No need to keep up as many physical classrooms, no need for faculty office space. Scheduling conflicts? Gone. The students will adjust; they are amazingly adaptable and resilient. But a whole way of educating may be on the brink of being lost.

I've adjusted to this new mode of teaching, using interactive Google Docs and fielding a lot of emails from students when they run into confusion or uncertainty, which is often.

It's been fine. I have one-on-one virtual appointments or phone calls with them whenever they request. Meanwhile, the increase in Zoom meetings for various committees has been almost debilitating: there's something about the psychological demands of the screen-bound grid that make me pine for the days of boring, wasteful committee meetings conducted in person. (At least I could zone out without having to see my visage displayed on a matrix of other always-alert faces!)

Will students come back to campuses in droves someday in the future, when a normal college education sounds like the perfect way to collectively reassert normalcy? Or will higher education face a massive adjustment, after which in-person teaching is relegated to the dustbin of history? I sure hope for the former. But digital technologies and the trends that they portend obviously suggest (and even prefer) the latter.

23

First-Year Seminar

One of the casualties of the pandemic online/hybrid teaching was the experience of first-year seminars: those (ideally) smaller, mixed-discipline classes that aim to give freshmen an orientation not just to a specific subject (though that is supposed to happen, too) but also to general college survival strategies, research methods, and the like.

The pragmatic reason that many colleges and universities require something like a first-year seminar is *retention*, or keeping students enrolled from semester to semester. Such courses have been shown to improve retention rates, especially over the critical fall to spring in a student's first year. These courses did not really translate on a mass scale to online delivery or hybrid models, because their high-contact purpose was compromised by the low-contact (if not *no*-contact) necessities of the Covid pandemic.

Having taught several of these courses over the past decade or so, I've experienced them at their peak efficacy. But I've also seen how administrative nickel-and-diming can negatively impact first-year seminars, rendering them pointless in some cases and even counterproductive in others.

I never took such a course, when I was in college. Or rather, *all* my first-year courses functioned like this, in a sense: at my small liberal arts school freshmen were enrolled almost exclusively in *freshman* classes, the introductory courses in a variety of subjects. Our classmates were similarly disoriented, newly arrived peers. Of course, my professors for the most part could not have cared less about "orienting" us to college: they were there in their corduroy blazers with leather elbow patches to "profess" to us, as one particularly sneering, Snape-like history professor told us the first day of class. (He would later take me to his office one day after class, draw a circle on his office chalkboard with a "T" [for Truth] in the middle, and explain to me that I was either *in* the circle or *out*. He was an intense sort of Christian. It was a weird office hour. It probably left a scar that made me highly sensitized to not intimidating my students.) Still, those first-year courses at Hillsdale College managed to be a group experience, giving us things to bond over and work through—even if the classes were not set up to nurture, exactly.

Today's first-year experience is supposed to be equal parts college-class and support mechanism for delicate new students. I'm not saying "delicate" sarcastically: the rate of cultural acceleration combined with intensifying socioeconomic pressures creates the conditions for twenty-first-century students to be especially delicate, and in highly varied ways. The aim of the first-year seminar is to provide an academic base, but *base* in the sense of homebase or homeroom even—a familiar context where students can find comfort and familiarity in the fray of the first year away at college.

I've periodically seen these seminars backfire for some students who are local and still live at home; they not only feel like they don't *need* this support system but feel like it's an expensive obstacle or imposition for them, on the way to just getting their other required classes out of the way. The first-year seminar model is geared toward students who are away from home (maybe far away, maybe for the first time) and for whom a small seminar with other first-years can be grounding, both academically and in terms of coping with day-to-day life.

I've started to embrace this latter model more and more, even as I recognize that it's not for every kind of student, and that it arguably degrades the intellectual content of first-year courses. But for those who really need it, I do believe a small multidisciplinary first-year seminar is an invaluable experience. In these seminars I may ask my students to read a short story, or I might hand out a poem to read together in class; but often I'll start the day with some broad questions, like "How's everyone doing? Any issues coming up with your other classes? What questions do you have for me?"—and usually at least one student will have something that's bothering them or confusing them, and a conversation will ensue . . . the goal being not just to help that one student deal with what is often a decidedly *non*academic problem but to foster the beginnings of a community of learners. We're all in this together, and by performing it we make it so.

These classes can be awkward because the students are from different disciplines (or haven't yet a clue what their "discipline" is) and so half the struggle is just getting them to open up and talk with one another. One thing I do whenever I can is to bring bags of satsuma mandarins to class. These are delicious when they're in season, and some students not from the region have never had one— never unpeeled the soft skin from green fruit to discover the sweet juicy flesh inside. More local students have eaten them throughout their lives but maybe not in a couple years. I pass the bag around at the beginning of class—not everyone takes one, which is fine— and we eat them as we sort out preliminary matters. (Writing this paragraph now, in December 2020, it feels like a lifetime ago: sitting around a seminar table unmasked, passing a communal bag of fruit around, snacking together in close proximity . . . ha!)

This sharing may sound precious or just incidental to pedagogy, but food insecurity is a real thing for many students. One piece of fruit does not solve this problem, but it acknowledges that food matters, and that not all of us have as much as we should. It's also a simple pleasure and starts off a class with a bit of joy.

I fondly remember my graduate seminars with Marc Blanchard, at UC Davis. Marc was a student of Michel Foucault and taught a class on the works of Foucault that positively channeled his spirit, without ever becoming regurgitative or hagiographic. One class early in the quarter, Marc brought a bag of edamame and a bottle of malbec to our class (it was an evening seminar). We sat there discussing *The Archaeology of Knowledge* while sipping little plastic cups of red wine and munching the soybeans. It was a minor epiphany for me, this simple gesture of adding something to snack on during class. So I've adapted this practice for my classes at Loyola and try to bring in satsumas or sometimes apples or small sweet peppers.

I'm mentioning this here in my discussion of first-year seminars because eating and hydration are real issues that are often not discussed outside of dorms or nonacademic student support contexts (if at all). As we eat our mandarins, we can also talk about where to *get* mandarins (local farmers' markets) and where they get their food on and off campus. We can edge toward talking about staying hydrated and why not to mix different alcohols, should they find themselves in party situations. This might verge on sounding infantilizing, but I have found that my students are relieved to have a context in which to discuss these things that is somewhere between just-with-friends and in a structured advice or counseling-type scenario. In our class we can keep it lighthearted while also offering practical tips and serious wisdom: the best deal off campus for a po-boy sandwich, how much coffee you can drink without going berserk, what kind of teas are good for upset stomachs, or in lieu of coffee. . . . And these turn into other questions: Where is the best place to study, on campus? How *does* one study, in the first place? How much sleep do we *really* need? How do you balance work and school? What if your living situation is untenable?

I'm always heartened to see how my students come together to brainstorm these matters of mere survival or adapting to university life. This kind of easy entry into the everyday class session can then surprisingly shift into talking about whatever formal text or topic is under discussion. And the students are thus learning not just about a subject but about this experience of living called being an adult, in college.

Two of the biggest threats to this kind of seminar are the class size and the type of instructor employed to teach the course. If the class size gets much bigger than fifteen, the seminar atmosphere cannot be sustained. The difference between a class of fifteen and a class of twenty is profound; twenty-five is a whole other category, and thirty is in another universe. (I realize I'm focusing here on a kind of small class sizes that some students *never* experience, in certain larger university settings. And I do recognize that many professors are excellent lecturers in larger settings and that it can be an equally stimulating way to learn; I assisted several professors at UC Davis in such undergraduate lectures. Here, though, I'm just reflecting on the small seminar as a first-year undergraduate experience.)

When administrators push class sizes up to and then past twenty, in order to cut costs, the special first-year experience is compromised— the kind of intimate discussion and bonding made possible by a smaller group dissipates with each added student, each extra seat in the class. This is no one's fault alone, but just the reality of effort it takes—for the instructor and all students—to hold the class in a collective mind space, attending to one another with respect and care and making shared intellectual breakthroughs.

These courses are also benefited by being taught by tenured or tenure-track faculty, as the kind of subject areas that ignite student interest tend to be fueled by long research projects and with intellectual and creative risk taking that is institutionally protected by academic freedom. In addition, the most effective way for these seminars to work is when students encounter a faculty member who will likely be teaching future advanced courses that the student may want to take ... following up on material from the first-year seminar. Students may even end up working closely with their first-year seminar professors on senior theses or other capstone activities. (I've had this experience dozens of times over the years, working with students at the end of their college careers—and even beyond—after meeting them at first in first-year courses.)

As passionate and devoted as an adjunct or contingent instructor may be—and most are, as teachers!—they usually lack any firm commitment from the institution that they will be there long term. And even if they are, they will often teach a specified and relatively static set of courses, and often not extending past general education or introductory material. Further, contingent faculty contracts often explicitly exclude one-on-one work with students; it's neither expected nor compensated. Finally, these faculty are not hired for their active research agendas; they are hired *only* to teach. I stress that *only* because it reveals how an institution can undervalue the connection between research and teaching—as if they can be so easily separated or as if they *should* be. While certainly some adjunct instructors may be fresh out of graduate school and still working on their own projects, contingent teaching positions are not expected to push the edges of a discipline or necessarily experiment with new methods of teaching and collaborative research. (Not that tenured faculty are necessarily prone to trying new things! And tenure-track faculty may be rightfully nervous to draw unwanted attention to radical pedagogical methods. But these are different challenges, for another book.)

In short, when institutions increase class size and rely on contingent faculty to staff first-year seminars, these factors undermine how such classes are intended to function, at their best. And unfortunately, these are the trends at many institutions, including my own. After the pandemic, what will be the status of first-year seminars? Will they be lost in the scrum of a prolonged recovery? Or might they be reclaimed as the special transition experiences they are, as soft and squishy entrance portals into the real work of, well, *real* higher education?

24

Pitt's Law

One first-year seminar I proposed was rejected by the selection committee at my school: it was going to be on Brad Pitt. I thought it would be an engaging and entertaining way to teach students how philosophical concepts and textures exist right on the surface of culture and around our most popular figures. But the committee scoffed at my proposal, so that seminar never happened. Maybe for the better, but I'm not sure.

In the long months of the Covid pandemic, we needed any good news we could get. And so, on Monday April 13, 2020, we got Brad Pitt providing an act of kindness in the guise of a reality show: Pitt had challenged TV stars the Property Brothers, for the premiere of their new show *Celebrity IOU*, to renovate the garage of his longtime makeup artist, Jean Black. The results were moving and moved across social media feeds in turn.

Pitt, of course, is known for dabbling in design and for his keen interest in architecture, even if sometimes the results have been tarnished by realities on the ground—such as in the case of his Make it Right homes in the Lower Ninth Ward of New Orleans, a still unraveling travesty that makes local news headlines from time to time.

If this touching breath of fresh air on *Celebrity IOU* arrived welcomingly during our 2020 quarantines, it wasn't the first instance that we'd been enamored with Pitt in recent times. Before the pandemic closed most things down, Donald Trump was at a rally in Colorado Springs, ranting about the Academy Awards, when he took a jab at Brad Pitt: "And then you have Brad Pitt, I was never a big fan of his. He got up, said a little wise guy thing. He's a little wise guy." This was an apparent reference to Pitt's Oscar acceptance speech quip concerning the Senate, which failed to "do the right thing" with respect to Trump's first impeachment trial. Both these statements swirled around the internet, Trump and Pitt two sides of the same viral currency.

There's an adage about the internet called Poe's Law: without context and with context itself constantly shifting, it's impossible to know whether a statement—or image, meme, or GIF—is intended seriously or ironically. Poe's Law governs every exchange over text messages, Twitter posts, comment threads. . . . It's part of the maddeningly seductive labyrinth that comprises this communicative landscape.

I thought about Poe's Law in this time of the coronavirus when I noticed on the CNN site an ad for an app called Starz, featuring the latest Quentin Tarantino film *Once Upon a Time . . . in Hollywood* with Leonardo DiCaprio on the side and Brad Pitt directly in the middle of the frame, mugging in all their 1969 period glory. Weirdly, Pitt was wearing the same Hawaiian shirt he wore in a scene from the Property Brothers episode—creating a curious Möbius strip of Hollywood fiction and reality TV, a past era and the tense present.

Below this ad spot was a secondary ad for a CNN podcast called "CORONAVIRUS: FACT VS. FICTION"—with the by-then ubiquitous topographical close-up of the spherical virus with spurs, in high definition. I was struck by the proximity of Hollywood entertainment (and specifically, a filmic spectacle that dabbles in revisionist history) above the supposed seriousness of understanding this virus from a scientific vantage point. But these two items are rendered equally clickable. Fact or fiction, life or death, just a bit of entertainment—who's to know? It's Poe's Law, in a nutshell.

The CNN adscape formed an uncanny juxtaposition, and it exposed a weird, unsettling truth about the moment: while so much changed over 2020—and will continue to change, in the coming years—there are also tenacious cultural habits in place that are refusing to change. As if a quasi-scientific podcast that zooms precisely into the scale of the virus could possibly clear everything up for us in this moment. As if reveling in a couple hours of Brad Pitt's grit can salve this vast, gaping wound that is us. In fact, Brad Pitt's renewed life on the screen, of late—and on *all* our screens, thanks to social media—suggests a new adage: *Pitt's Law*.

Pitt's Law might be defined as a widespread craving for "more of the same." When pastiche, parody, satire, and collage lack useful distinction, all that matters is that the swirling parts—Pitt's parts, most vividly—are kept in recognizable, safe shape. More Brad Pitt doing what Brad Pitt does. Brad Pitt was able to slay the zombie apocalypse, avert the Manson murders, and singlehandedly decimate the Nazis; could *he* be the silver bullet for the novel coronavirus, or at least for a return to normalcy? The tantalizing image of Jean Black's remodeled garage suggested so—if obliquely. *Saturday Night Live* cleverly cast Pitt as Dr. Anthony Fauci in a magical fusion of hilarity and homage. Then Pitt even narrated an ad spot for Joe Biden, in the final run-up to the election.

I should admit something, maybe something I should have disclosed earlier: for a long time I've been a sucker for anything Brad Pitt. I coedited an academic book about him several years ago called *Deconstructing Brad Pitt*, to the amusement (maybe horror) of some of my colleagues. Pitt's performances have always fascinated me for how they challenge standard ideas of heteronormative white masculinity in Western culture—even as the actor is, on the surface, an embodiment of the very stereotypes his roles often subvert. Pitt's characters are clever, articulate, and edgy, but always with a healthy dose of critical self-awareness, sometimes even self-destructiveness. He takes interest in how real things are constructed, and he is comfortable wearing a dress, as he did for *Rolling Stone* in 1999.

My interest was piqued anew by a *New Yorker* article from 2019 in which director James Gray discussed working with Pitt on the meticulous scene choreography for *Ad Astra*. And then Pitt's performance in Tarantino's *Once Upon a Time . . . in Hollywood* won an Academy Award. It seemed as though Pitt had not only made a strong comeback from his announced retirement a few years prior, but that his characters had acquired even more depth and nuance.

Pitt's visage and clever quips during his award speeches have been all over social media: whipping up fresh speculations about his friendship with ex-wife Jennifer Aniston, reviving his sex appeal and causing entertainment writers to wonder what is truly going on with Pitt.

But after watching both of the new films, I found myself flummoxed. Pitt's latest resurgence in popularity was perhaps most surprising because, well, the performances in his two 2019 films were so unsurprising. (Unlike the somewhat still recent *War Machine*, which was a masterpiece of acting.) As stuntman Cliff Booth in *Once Upon a Time . . . in Hollywood*, Pitt's trajectory from eccentrically charming sidekick to unflinching muscleman recalls so many earlier Pitt performances that culminate in spectacular violence—think of *Snatch* and *Fight Club*, to name just two examples. Audiences admire the physical beauty of Pitt, his brute strength and his ability to inflict severe vengeance.

Tarantino's reuse of this pattern is hardly innovative. And while it may be comfortably familiar to watch Pitt re-emerge as the goofy, vicious agent of redemptive violence, it's also chilling. Here we are in the age of toxic masculinity correction, amid the stubborn, drawn-out crumbling of white patriarchy, and we still need to see a merciless Brad Pitt—spoiler alert—smash apart the head of a female character? My fandom has its limits.

Ad Astra stars Pitt in what can only be an almost nonfictional role, with voice-overs reflecting on his neglect of people in his life, those he has hurt, family ties severed, loved ones lost, and other personal failings. It's hard not to hear Pitt himself processing his own years of domestic struggle and anguish. Director James Gray described these voice-overs as "a constant ongoing soliloquy" running throughout the film. Amid interviews and profiles reflecting on Pitt's own drama, it's all but impossible to detach Pitt's role in *Ad Astra* from his real-life revelations and breakthroughs. I'm not sneering here; it was strangely refreshing to see such emotional earnestness mirrored on screen.

So *Ad Astra* is, overwhelmingly, a movie about *Brad Pitt*. About Brad Pitt in space (where he *always* is, strictly speaking), reckoning with solitude while simultaneously charged with being his best self and getting clean so that he might save the entire planet. It's a preposterous mission, yet one that is all too palatable: that *one man* can revise history (Pitt's Cliff Booth), can make a country great again (Donald Trump), can save all humankind (Jesus, Elon Musk).

In *Once Upon a Time . . . in Hollywood*, Tarantino composed Pitt's various expressions, moves, and affects into a set piece, as if through it we might see Pitt's own filmography. It's no wonder that Pitt ended his Oscar acceptance speech by quoting the film's title: "Once upon a time in Hollywood—ain't that the truth." Yet it seemed clear to me that Pitt's Oscar was really more of a lifetime achievement award; they just didn't call it that, as if they weren't sure we'd be around for another year to give such an award. *Ad Astra* was after all, in an uncanny coincidence, premised on such imminent doom: as the Anthropocene looms larger each year, human triumphs become a harbinger of imminent planetary catastrophe. It might come from mysterious rays coming from Neptune; or it might arrive in the form of a virus already on Earth.

Either way, the appearance of Pitt embodies an ambient hope for more of the same. The *Once Upon a Time . . . in Hollywood* film poster subtitle—"The 9th film from Quentin Tarantino"—made this plain: what mattered was *quantity*, not quality. Just keep 'em coming.

Pitt's latest roles express a tenacious nostalgia for times past— not just the late 1960s but the 1990s for Tarantino and Pitt—and a somber premonition concerning a near future in ruins. These are the end games of our current moment, or just after: longing for the past, terrified of the future. Watching these films was like looking through some sort of bizarre multisensory kaleidoscope and occasionally seeing and hearing Pitt's personae refracted and recycled, to a dizzying extent—as if to reassure that things might still be the same. Or that we could bring back a reliable actor/builder to help us renovate the present. If not Pitt, then maybe Val Kilmer? (No, probably not.)

What I saw in *Once Upon a Time . . . in Hollywood* and in *Ad Astra* was an unsettling, unquenchable thirst for Brad Pitt, *any* Brad Pitt, as long as he squares with something we've known, something we wish we could get back to—something long gone, for better or worse. Or maybe really for the better, if only we could let go of Pitt's Law. If we could truly open up, not to more the same but to building something new. I think even Brad Pitt would like that. And now in the long outstretching months of Covid-19, *the same* is no longer even an option. Pitt's Law may have announced itself only in time to be broken for good.

I'm including this chapter in my book partly as a reminder to myself: I'm not simply pining for something I experienced in the 1990s, I'm not lamenting an educational experience as if we could easily revert to it. I'm open to something new. But I'm also taking stock of where we've gone, what we've been doing, in the meantime . . . this drawing out of the hopes and nightmares of the recent past.

25

Into the Unknown

As I near the end of this book, I realize that there are still so many observations and anecdotes I wanted to include. So many experiences teaching and learning during the first twenty years of the twenty-first century, so many illuminations I've had and connections I've made along the way. But the book has to end somewhere, and I wanted this book to be a short book (again, a *Gatsby*!) about teaching in the humanities in higher education these days . . . even as "these days" morphed into altogether new days, what with the Covid pandemic changing life on campus dramatically and with its long effects still unclear. But what is clear is that there is no going back, even to things that I'd like to recover.

In many ways I consider this book a follow-up to my earlier book *The Work of Literature in an Age of Post-Truth*. So this is the next installment of my reflections on teaching. Sometimes I feel hopeless, exhausted by the techno-cultural whirlwind of digital life and dismayed by the administrative bloat and cynical data-driven positivism that rule most discourse about higher education as more and more of it merges into the online ether. Other times I still manage to feel the thrill of learning, the rush of uncertainty at the edge of a breakthrough. To quote Anand Pandian from his book *A Possible Anthropology: Methods for Uneasy Times*, "This paradoxical complicity between teaching and *un*knowing is . . . not without its hazards." And yet to feel this *with* my students . . . this is what keeps me going.

*   *   *

So strange an accident has happened to us, that I cannot forbear recording it . . .

One day early in the term in my first-year English class in fall 2018 we were discussing the opening of Mary Shelley's *Frankenstein*, and almost immediately the conversation turned to *this Robert Walton guy*: Who the heck *is* he? Weren't we supposed to be reading about some dude named Frankenstein? One student asked why Walton signs each of his first three letters differently: R. Walton, then Robert Walton, and finally R.W.

I asked: Are we saying that Walton's identity—and the whole book, maybe—is a bit wobbly, right off the bat? Another student wondered: What is this map doing before the title page? I'd read this novel six or seven times before, but had never given the map, with its straight edges and embossed place-names, serious attention before now. A map suggests we *know* the place, several students replied; we *control* it—or we *desire* to control it. Why might a map be of use as we begin (or even *before* we begin) this novel? Well, we know that Robert Walton is on a journey, off to discover a north passage. Exploration is in the air. And on the page.

But the map that precedes the text of *Frankenstein* is strange: it doesn't even come close to the north passage, where the book ostensibly begins. It accounts for a *later* geography in the novel, the area around Lake Geneva. Our conversation was fast-paced, complex, spontaneous, and exciting. I hadn't planned for or predicted any of it. Our allotted fifty minutes flew by. It was a dream class, and yet just an ordinary class, pre-pandemic: sitting in a jagged circle; the invariably awkward start of the conversation; embarrassing silences—all of us fumbling toward knowledge, confronted with something to read, interpret, *learn* something about.

It was also pre-registration time, which meant I was advising students on how to navigate their paths to graduation. I had been noticing that more and more of them were saying, "Well, I *guess* I'll take an online class or two . . ." This was code, I gradually realized, for not having to *go* to class. It's a concession, of sorts. But it was also ambivalent: like, they knew they weren't going to get the same quality experience, even though it might be "easier" in a strict sense of not having to be physically *in* a classroom. This was understandable: many of my students work multiple jobs to pay for tuition and are pressed for time. Online classes are delivered to them via their computers, their mobile phones. *Delivery*: that's what administrators and support staff call it. Uber but for education, or as if one's learning will arrive in a box festooned with the semiotics of Amazon Prime or FedEx.

Online courses cost the same. For instance, a student at my university pays the exact same tuition for an eight-week online composition course as the same semester-long composition course "on the ground" (or "face-to-face," depending on your institution). And an online course's goals and outcomes are supposed to be the same as those offered on the physical campus. But most instructors will admit that the online experience is not at all the same as being in a classroom with students. And many will even confess that learning in online courses is patently inferior to learning face-to-face.

I asked my students about this. The word "conversation" came up many times as they talked about online classes, as the key part that was missing. Here is a direct quote from one of my students: "There's so much pressure to have something formalized, which completely misses the point of conversation." That is, while the expectations for discussion in an online class are in some ways higher, because they comprise some formal part of the grade, the online version of class discussion can't compete with the real thing in terms of quality and nuance.

Online courses are usually mapped out clearly in advance. From the perspective of curriculum committees or strategic planning groups, I can see how they are attractive. But these classes, no matter how tightly designed and smartly conceived, can never deliver the magic of conversation—the energy and community dynamic such as I experienced teaching *Frankenstein* that day. To paraphrase what Maria Bustillos wrote for *The Verge* in 2013 after taking a well-respected MOOC herself: online courses can be a lot of things, but what they aren't is *college*.

I'm not trying to set up or maintain a simplistic dichotomy between online classes and on-the-ground classes; I once naively tried to do that at *Inside Higher Ed*, and I got a lot of flak for it in the comments after the piece—which ironically reflected the worst of the web in their very attempts to counter my claims about the limits of internet communication. And in the year that I am finishing this book, of course, I'm teaching entirely online myself—I'm acutely aware that virtual classrooms and remote teaching tools are, in many ways, the new normal.

There are innumerable ways, good and bad, to teach both online and in a traditional classroom. But giving students the as-if neutral alternative of online learning can result in an institutionalized depreciation of the actual classroom. And not just the classroom in general but of the kinds of unscripted, serendipitous conversations that can still happen in these spaces. The sincere excitement and pleasure of not knowing, but *learning*, together. The unpredictable, live, social production of knowledge: bodies squirming in seats, uncertain minds on edge, overcoming shyness to jump in: it feels all the more rare, and almost mystical, as online offerings are made equivalent and not just supplemental to classes on the ground.

Classroom learning requires experiences of uncertainty, drawn out for seconds or even minutes—sometimes an entire semester can feel off kilter—but we're increasingly accustomed to obliterating such time by reaching for our smartphones or tapping away from one screen to another. There, we can find everything we need—and plenty with which to kill time even when we *don't* know what we need; phones have become appendages, natural extensions of our bodies, and we use them to neutralize all the in-between moments in life: waiting for food to arrive; as passengers on airplanes; before the light turns green, in our driver's seats; walking across campus . . .

And at this point, smartphones have thoroughly infiltrated the classroom. College students using their phones during class are not necessarily being defiant or rebellious; more and more, they don't even try to hide their phones when they tap at them mid-class. They're not ashamed. It's just life, what they've grown up into. But it is becoming increasingly difficult for them to pay sustained attention in order to participate in class—to head willingly "into the unknown" (to borrow from Queen Elsa, our contemporary explorer of the mythical north).

Most institutions these days offer (and even require) online learning management platforms such as Blackboard or Canvas. As discussed earlier, these systems allow instructors and students to upload and access course materials, and conduct discussions—outside of, in tandem with, or even comprising class. They also accommodate grading and feedback. The automation enforced by these platforms mirrors the spread of platforms and apps throughout every aspect of life, from banking and shopping to medical records, social media, and news delivery.

Despite having grown up online, my students have no love for these platforms. They're not sold on the efficiencies promised by Blackboard or Canvas. At best, they just *work*. These things rapidly become just another app to keep track of, another website to log on to late at night, another password to forget. The Blackboard or Canvas app is for my students some kind of pre-work work vortex, just one more layer of drudgery in a hellscape of never-ending digital labor.

The slickly designed, familiar chat-box cascade on an LMS seems to formalize and standardize conversation—and invite more voices in, even!—but ends up feeling halting, intimidating, and ultimately like a wretched simulacrum. One of my students observed, "The more sophisticated your responses are, the less likely other classmates will engage with them." My students say they feel more pressure to produce content for these online discussion boards, even when they have lower expectations for the results of the exchange. A lot of students expressed something like a numb acceptance of these platforms, which to be honest I found a bit rattling.

"It's the Devil we know," one student concluded, rather chillingly.

Blackboard and Canvas and their ilk, when adopted and normalized by institutions, make *all* learning contexts *online* learning contexts, to some extent. What matters is the continuous flow of *content* through the platforms. Fill up the Blackboard, paint the Canvas. The platform is indifferent as to whether the class meets in person or only online, as long as the virut folders and subfolders are filled and accessed, files downloaded and uploaded. Sometimes there might be a discussion board, threads about a certain reading or assignment. But, as my students hinted, don't confuse this with a *conversation*.

Students also mentioned their discomfort with the surveillance aspect of Blackboard, which registers when they are online, when and for how long they take a quiz, and so on. I hadn't thought about this before, but what use is being made of this information, who is selling it, why and to whom?

*   *   *

Handwriting in terrible script written in real chalk on the Blackboard; awkward lapses after a question has been raised; writing together in the moment, on pieces of paper—these things feel clumsy and slow compared to the digital educational utopia, compared with the little rectangular supercomputers in our pockets, compared with the procedural sublime of online interfaces and their promises of data-driven achievement and clear measurability.

But there's something profoundly humbling about being in a classroom with other learners, and with a teacher, actually learning. At its best, it's always an experience of venturing into the unknown.

There's really no map for it, no way to measure it in the moment. It's an ineffable yet crucial part of the learning experience. And it's something that online learning platforms *and* smartphones mitigate, if in competing ways. The classroom interrupts the normal patterns of activity—specifically with regard to being online, creating and consuming content. Conversations gum up the works—so we might change our perspectives, think differently, get stumped. So we might experience a pedagogy of the depressed.

In the classroom we are reminded daily of the processual, meandering, stop-and-start nature of learning. Its *human* aspect, its paths of mystery and surprise. The unknown is right here, in the real classroom, and we must not lose sight of it. Maybe I have fallen back into a dualistic position, here, arguing for the inestimable value of "face-to-face" conversations and "on-the-ground" classrooms, against the new digital ecosystem of online learning. But if conversations dry up, any value all that educational content may have had will evaporate with them. "Online learning" and all its elaborate apparatus will turn out to have been a false paradise—not so unlike Robert Walton's imagined temperate climes of the far north.

Reprint Acknowledgments

"No Place Like Home" at *Popula*
"Trigger U." at *The Honest Ulsterman*
"Ecophobia" at *Popula*
"Teaching Critical Theory Today" at *Inside Higher Ed*
"Turning Kids into Capital" at *Public Books*
"Into the Unknown" at *Popula*

Bibliography

Barthes, Roland. *Roland Barthes*. Hill and Wang, 2010.

Berlant, Lauren, and Kathleen Stewart. *The Hundreds*. Duke University Press, 2019.

Biss, Eula. *Having and Being Had*. Riverhead, 2020.

Cohen, Jeffrey Jerome. *Prismatic Ecology: Ecotheory Beyond Green*. University of Minnesota Press, 2014.

Corin, Lucy. *The Entire Predicament*. Tin House Books, 2007.

Eklund, Hillary, ed. *Ground-Work: English Renaissance Literature and Soil Science*. Duquesne University Press, 2017.

Estok, Simon C. *The Ecophobia Hypothesis*. Routledge, 2018.

Fitzpatrick, Kathleen. *Generous Thinking*. Johns Hopkins University Press, 2018.

Haraway, Donna Jeanne. "A Manifesto for Cyborgs." In *The Routledge Critical and Cultural Theory Reader*, edited by Neil Badmington, 324–55. Thomas, 2008.

Harris, Malcolm. *Kids These Days: Human Capital and the Making of Millennials*. Little Brown and Company, 2018.

Messeri, Lisa. *Placing Outer Space: An Earthly Ethnography of Other Worlds*. Duke University Press, 2016.

Nelson, Maggie. *Shiner*. Hanging Loose Press, 2001.

Nelson, Maggie. *Something Bright, Then Holes*. Soft Skull Press, 2007.

Nelson, Maggie. *Bluets*. Wave Books, 2009.

Nelson, Maggie. *The Argonauts*. Graywolf Press, 2016.

Nelson, Maggie. *The Red Parts: Autobiography of a Trial*. Graywolf Press, 2016.

Pandian, Anand. *A Possible Anthropology: Methods for Uneasy Times*. Duke University Press, 2019.

Rankine, Claudia. *Just Us*. Graywolf, 2020.

Said, Edward. *Beginnings: Intention and Method*. Granta, 1975.

Said, Edward. *Orientalism*. Vintage Books, 2004.

Schaberg, Christopher. *The Textual Life of Airports: Reading the Culture of Flight*. Bloomsbury Academic, 2013.

Schaberg, Christopher. *The End of Airports*. Bloomsbury Academic, 2015.

Schaberg, Christopher. *Airportness: The Nature of Flight*. Bloomsbury
  Academic, 2017.
Schaberg, Christopher. *Searching for the Anthropocene: A Journey into the
  Environmental Humanities*. Bloomsbury Academic, 2019.
Schaberg, Christopher, and Robert Bennet, eds. *Deconstructing Brad Pitt*.
  Bloomsbury, 2014.
Scharmen, Fred. *Space Settlements*. Columbia University, 2019.
Shelley, Mary. Frankenstein. Norton, 2011.
Stewart, Kathleen. *Ordinary Affects*. Duke University Press, 2007.
Williams, John. *Stoner*. New York Review Books, 2006.
Woolf, Virginia. *Orlando: A Biography*. Harcourt Brace and Co, 1993.

Films and Television

Fincher, David, dir. *Fight Club*. 20th Century Fox, 1999.
Goldblum, Jeff, et al. *The World According to Jeff Goldblum*. Disney+,
  November 12, 2019.
Gray, James, dir. *Ad Astra*. 20th Century Fox, 2019.
Jonze, Spike, dir. *Her*. Annapurna Pictures, 2013.
Kershner, Irvin, dir. *The Empire Strikes Back*. 20th Century Fox, 1980.
The Mandalorian. Created by Jon Favreau. Disney+, November 12, 2019.
Marquand, Richard, dir. *Return of the Jedi*. 20th Century Fox, 1983.
Ritchie, Guy, dir. *Snatch*. Sony Pictures Releasing, 2000.
Tarantino, Quentin, dir. *Once Upon a Time . . . in Hollywood*. Sony Pictures
  Releasing, 2019.
Wachowski, Lana, and Wachowski, Lilly, dirs. *The Matrix*. Warner Bros.
  Pictures, 1999.

Web Resources

@JustinNystrom. "Somehow Having a tv Show Film a Fake Shooting Scene
  Outside My Office Is Screwing with Me. Was It Being at Virginia Tech in
  2007? Oh Right, Right. It Is That." *Twitter*, November 8, 2019, 9:37 a.m.
  https://twitter.com/JustinNystrom/status/1192828408935440384.

@nbcsnl. "And now, a Message from Dr. Anthony Fauci. #SNLAtHome." *Twitter*, April 25, 2020, 10:35 p.m. https://twitter.com/nbcsnl/status/1 254252640399249408.

"1999 Rolling Stone Covers." *Rolling Stone*. Rolling Stone, June 25, 2018. www.rollingstone.com/music/music-lists/1999-rolling-stone-covers-216141/rs-824-brad-pitt-49689/.

"Active Shooter Preparedness." *Loyola University New Orleans Emergency Information Site*. Loyola University New Orleans. emergency.loyno.edu/active-shooter-preparedness.

Allison, Sarah. "Harry Potter's Scar, or Book Recs from a Columbine Grad." *Public Books*, April 20, 2018. www.publicbooks.org/harry-potters-scar-or-book-recs-from-a-columbine-grad/.

"Assistant Professor of Global Digital and Televisual/Video Cultures." *Brown*. Brown University. apply.interfolio.com/51717.

Aviv, Rachel. "The Philosopher of Feelings." *The New Yorker*, July 18, 2018. www.newyorker.com/magazine/2016/07/25/martha-nussbaums-moral-philosophies.

Beresford, Trilby. "Trump Rips 'Parasite' Oscars Win and Brad Pitt in Colorado Rally Rant." *The Hollywood Reporter*, February 20, 2020. www.hollywoodreporter.com/news/trump-takes-aim-at-parasite-oscars-win-brad-pitt-colorado-rally-rant-1280306.

Brodesser-akner, Taffy. "What Happened to Val Kilmer? He's Just Starting to Figure It Out." *The New York Times*, The New York Times, May 6, 2020. www.nytimes.com/2020/05/06/magazine/val-kilmer.html.

Bustillos, Maria. "Online Classes Can Be Enlightening, Edifying, and Engaging—but They're Not College." *The Verge*, May 28, 2013. www.theverge.com/2013/5/28/4363450/online-classes-can-be-enlightening-but-moocs-arent-college.

Carillo, Ellen C., et al. "Public Humanities." *MLA Profession*, 2019. profession.mla.org/issue/public-humanities/.

Corbett, Kelly. "Brad Pitt Surprises His Makeup Artist With Guest House Makeover in 'Celebrity IOU.'" *House Beautiful*, House Beautiful, April 14, 2020. www.housebeautiful.com/design-inspiration/home-makeovers/a32105807/celebrity-iou-premiere-brad-pitt-jean-black/.

Chu, Andrea Long. "I Worked with Avital Ronell. I Believe Her Accuser." *The Chronicle of Higher Education*, The Chronicle of Higher Education,

August 30, 2018. www.chronicle.com/article/I-Worked-With-Avital-Ron ell-I/244415/.

Davidson, Nikki. "Where Did All the Little Brown Lizards Come from?" *Wwltv.com*, September 13, 2019. www.wwltv.com/article/news/local/ where-did-all-the-little-brown-lizards-come-from-around-new-orleans /289-6d4c071b-5c06-40b8-bd24-2accc7338aa2.

Davison, Nicola. "The Anthropocene Epoch: Have We Entered a New Phase of Planetary History?" *The Guardian*, Guardian News and Media, May 30, 2019. www.theguardian.com/environment/2019/may/30/anthro pocene-epoch-have-we-entered-a-new-phase-of-planetary-history.

Fetters, Ashley. "Toward a Universal Theory of 'Mom Jeans.'" *The Atlantic*, Atlantic Media Company, August 28, 2019. www.theatlantic.com/family/ archive/2019/08/how-mom-jeans-became-cool-again/596992/.

Foucault, Michel. "'Panopticism' from 'Discipline & Punish: The Birth of the Prison.'" *Race/Ethnicity: Multidisciplinary Global Contexts* 2, no. 1 (2008): 1–12. JSTOR, www.jstor.org/stable/25594995. Accessed June 12, 2020.

Heller, Nathan. "The Man Who Sent Brad Pitt into Space." *The New Yorker*, September 9, 2019. www.newyorker.com/magazine/2019/09/16/james-g rays-journey-from-the-outer-boroughs-to-outer-space.

"Jennifer Aniston Posts Sexy Picture after Night Out with Ex Brad Pitt." *New Idea*, January 21, 2020. www.newidea.com.au/jennifer-aniston-post s-sexy-picture-after-night-out-with-ex-husband-brad-pitt.

King, Dianne. "Brad Pitt Says He'll Retire from in Front of the Camera When He Turns 50." *Daily Mail Online*, Associated Newspapers, November 15, 2011. www.dailymail.co.uk/tvshowbiz/article-2061122/ Brad-Pitt-says-hell-retire-camera-turns-50.html.

Kofman, Ava. "Bruno Latour, the Post-Truth Philosopher, Mounts a Defense of Science." *The New York Times*, The New York Times, October 25, 2018. www.nytimes.com/2018/10/25/magazine/bruno-latour-post-t ruth-philosopher-science.html.

Kolbert, Elizabeth. "Louisiana's Disappearing Coast." *The New Yorker*, March 25, 2019. www.newyorker.com/magazine/2019/04/01/louisianas -disappearing-coast.

Konstantinou, Lee. "Avital Ronell and the End of the Academic Star." *The Chronicle of Higher Education*, The Chronicle of Higher Education,

August 22, 2018. www.chronicle.com/article/Avital-Ronellthe-End
-of/244335?key=ZPRvPGcEksyNlrWwMqd4mthgZCOnSOCf-9BJcF5
ITaHDdgN6blsK8TdDsO6xPWkUbjBhNGZITW12a0FDRVhjUDFse
DlNRU80c0dCMmIwWS1CMVVqcG05U21YOA.

Lieberman, Mark. "Inside Higher Ed." *Inside Higher Ed*, March 14, 2018.
www.insidehighered.com/digital-learning/article/2018/03/14/experts-off
er-advice-convincing-faculty-members-teach-online-or.

Marchese, David. "Brad Pitt on the Kind of Leading Man He Doesn't Want to
Be." *The New York Times*, The New York Times, December 9, 2019. www
.nytimes.com/interactive/2019/12/09/magazine/brad-pitt-interview.html.

Marder, Michael. "The Coronavirus Is Us." *The New York Times*, The New
York Times, March 3, 2020. www.nytimes.com/2020/03/03/opinion/the
-coronavirus-is-us.html.

Melchior, Jillian Kay. "Opinion | Fake News Comes to Academia." *The Wall
Street Journal*, Dow Jones & Company, October 5, 2018. www.wsj.com/
articles/fake-news-comes-to-academia-1538520950.

Menza, Kaitlin. "Where Did Brad Pitt's Make It Right Foundation Go
Wrong?" *Architectural Digest*, January 18, 2019. www.architecturaldigest
.com/story/brad-pitt-make-it-right-foundation-new-orleans-katrina-l
awsuit.

Moore, Jason W. "The Capitalocene, Part I: On the Nature and Origins of
Our Ecological Crisis." *Taylor & Francis*, March 17, 2017. www.tandfo
nline.com/doi/abs/10.1080/03066150.2016.1235036?journalCode=fjps2
0.

Mounk, Yascha. "Cancel Everything." *The Atlantic*, Atlantic Media
Company, March 12, 2020. www.theatlantic.com/ideas/archive/2020/03/
coronavirus-cancel-everything/607675/.

O'Falt, Chris. "'I'm Not Kubrick': James Gray on the Hell of Filming Brad
Pitt Alone in a Black Box." *IndieWire*, IndieWire, September 27, 2019.
www.indiewire.com/2019/09/ad-astra-kubrick-2001-a-space-odyssey-j
ames-gray-filmmaker-toolkit-podcast-episode-92-1202176870/.

Phelps, Nicole. "The Metropolitan Museum of Art's Costume Institute
Announces Its 2020 Theme: About Time: Fashion and Duration." *Vogue*,
Vogue, November 7, 2019. www.vogue.com/article/costume-institute-
2020-exhibition-metgala-theme-about-time-fashion-duration.

"Pitt Falls for Lloyd Wright's Fallingwater." *TODAY.com*, December 8, 2006. www.today.com/id/16113827/ns/today-today_entertainment/t/pitt-falls -lloyd-wrights-fallingwater/#.XubaBzpKh1u.

Schaberg, Christopher. "Why I Won't Teach Online." *Inside Higher Ed*, Inside Higher Ed, March 7, 2018. www.insidehighered.com/digital-lear ning/views/2018/03/07/professor-explains-why-he-wont-teach-online -opinion.

Shea, Ryan. "Brad Pitt, 56, Looks Hotter Than Ever at the Producers Guild Awards in Los Angeles—See Pics." *Hollywood Life*, Hollywood Life, January 19, 2020. hollywoodlife.com/2020/01/19/brad-pitt-producers-g uild-awards-pics/.

Shelley, Percy Bysshe. "The Cloud by Percy Bysshe Shelley." *Poetry Foundation*, Poetry Foundation. www.poetryfoundation.org/poems /45117/the-cloud-56d2247bf4112.

Simonds, Sandra. "April." *The New Yorker*, The New Yorker, June 25, 2019. www.newyorker.com/magazine/2019/04/29/april.

Stommel, Jesse. "How to Ungrade." https://www.jessestommel.com/how-to -ungrade/.

Wallis, Stephen. "Brad Pitt and Frank Pollaro's Furniture Collection." *Architectural Digest*, Architectural Digest, December 1, 2012. www.a rchitecturaldigest.com/story/brad-pitt-frank-pollaro-furniture-collect ion-article.

Williams, Jeffrey. "The New Humanities." *The Chronicle of Higher Education*. https://www.chronicle.com/article/the-new-humanities/.

Wordsworth, William. "I Wandered Lonely as a Cloud by William Wordsworth." *Poetry Foundation*, Poetry Foundation. www.poetryfound ation.org/poems/45521/i-wandered-lonely-as-a-cloud.

Yahr, Emily. "America Has a Collective Weakness, and His Name Is Brad Pitt." *The Washington Post*, WP Company, February 5, 2020. www.w ashingtonpost.com/lifestyle/style/america-has-a-collective-weakness-an d-his-name-is-brad-pitt/2020/02/04/58340f6e-4781-11ea-8124-0ca81e ffcdfb_story.html.

Index

www.ingramcontent.com/pod-product-compliance
Ingram Content Group UK Ltd.
Pitfield, Milton Keynes, MK11 3LW, UK
UKHW031251020325
455690UK00007B/101